Reading's Non-Negotiables

Elements of Effective Reading Instruction

Rachael Gabriel

D1713956

ROWMAN & LITTLEFIELD EDUCATION
A division of
ROWMAN & LITTLEFIELD PUBLISHERS, INC.
Lanham • New York • Toronto • Plymouth, UK

Published by Rowman & Littlefield Education
A division of Rowman & Littlefield Publishers, Inc.
A wholly owned subsidiary of The Rowman & Littlefield Publishing Group, Inc.
4501 Forbes Boulevard, Suite 200, Lanham, Maryland 20706
www.rowman.com

10 Thornbury Road, Plymouth PL6 7PP, United Kingdom

British Library Cataloguing in Publication Information Available

Library of Congress Cataloging-in-Publication Data
Gabriel, Rachael E.
Reading's non-negotiables : elements of effective reading instruction / Rachael Gabriel.
p. cm.
Includes bibliographical references.
ISBN 978-1-4758-0116-3 (pbk. : alk. paper)—ISBN 978-1-4758-0117-0 (electronic)
1. Reading. I. Title.
LB1050.G23 2013
428.4—dc23
2012044865

™
The paper used in this publication meets the minimum requirements of American National Standard for Information Sciences Permanence of Paper for Printed Library Materials, ANSI/NISO Z39.48-1992.

Printed in the United States of America

Contents

Foreword

Rachael Gabriel's *Reading's Non-Negotiables* is a wonderful read! In this era when reductionism has once again taken over too much classroom instruction, Gabriel reminds readers about those things that really matter when it comes to developing students as active and engaged learners. She notes the research that supports reading instruction that is focused on accessing the meaning of the texts we read. At the same time she offers practical arguments for such instruction.

She does not argue that kids can teach themselves, but rather that when skills are taught and practiced in the context of actual text reading, students acquire the skills in a meaningful and useful way. Instruction that is wrapped in meaning and grounded in purpose, as Gabriel suggests, makes it more likely that students will be able to apply the skills they learn when they read. In other words, transfer of skills and knowledge to actual reading activity is easier for the students.

Gabriel emphasizes that, in the end, everyone agrees that good readers comprehend what they read. However, she also notes that classroom reading lessons and intervention lessons for struggling readers too often focus on things other than enhancing readers' understanding. She argues that every lesson in every subject area must have meaning-making as its primary goal.

While we need to worry about smaller issues such as word recognition accuracy, vocabulary acquisition fluency, and reading rate, when we lose sight of the ultimate goal—understanding what has been read—we can allocate too much time to the smaller pieces and undervalue developing proficiency and readers who understand what they read.

Tied to this understanding-focused model is motivation for learning which is fostered through a much wider use of self-selected texts and teacher demonstrations of the strategies that effective readers always use while reading, especially when reading texts that present obstacles to understanding. All students need easy access to texts they can read accurately, texts the also have an interest in reading. They benefit from writing activities that they find meaningful and benefit most when composing such texts occur daily.

Finally, Gabriel notes how potentially powerful literate conversations can be in classrooms focused on developing reading for understanding. Allowing, even encouraging, students to turn and talk to each other about their reading and writing is another classroom practice that is too often absent from too many classrooms. It is through such conversations that students acquire the subtle, and not so subtle, aspects of the subject matter they are studying. Silence, then, is not golden, at least in classrooms.

What Gabriel offers is a vision of what high-quality, evidence-based instruction could, and should, look like. Instead of a series of small and literal tasks to occupy students during the school day, she offers rich and complex tasks that support children as they develop into proficient readers and writers. I hope this book is read widely and that teachers take up the challenge Gabriel has established. That challenge—teaching all students in a more personal and complex environment—if met, will result in students who will become the literate citizens this nation needs to continue to move forward. So, read this book, and then, begin to alter the instruction youprovide in the several ways Gabriel suggests. The students are waiting.

Richard L. Allington, PhD
University of Tennessee

Preface

In the spring of 2012, Richard Allington and I wrote a brief article that outlined the non-negotiables described in this book. Over the weeks and months since its initial publication, we received more responses from teachers, principals, librarians, and other educators than we ever expected from a single article. Within them was a call for information and help for actualizing the ideas that resonated with so many readers. This book is a response to that call.

Reading 's Non-Negotiables is written for people engaged in the work of teaching reading who share a vision of instruction where literacy is always possible, always liberating, and in which students are viewed as already literate beings who come to school to make their literacies more evident and more powerful in their lives.

In the chapters that follow you will find an expanded discussion with examples and suggestions about seven non-negotiable elements of reading instruction. None of the examples or suggestions require additional resources—time, finances, or otherwise. They merely require adults to make the decision to do them. I hope that this book provides support for your work in the form of evidence from research, confirmation, and inspiration. I also hope it provides hope that the vision of every child reading is indeed within reach.

Happy reading,
Rachael Gabriel

Acknowledgments

I would like to thank Mia Abeles, Tammy Anderson, Alison Ashley, Lauren Bespuda, Kathy Evans, Mary Gabriel (Mom), Shannon Graham, Jessica Lester, and Ali Wilson for sharing their expertise and providing invaluable feedback on drafts of this text.

I would like to thank Hannah Dostal, my team's most valuable player, for her patient support, for teaching me about teaching, and for reminding me of what I know.

Finally, I would like to thank Dr. Allington for his generosity and guidance. I would not have been a reading teacher if I hadn't read his What Really Matters series, and I would not have become a researcher without his instruction: in class, in the field, and on the page. This book and many others exist because of his leadership and stubborn commitment to the coming reality of "every child a reader."

Introduction

Cycles of Reading Success

Instead of any one author's opinion of what is "best" (best practice, best program, best book about reading) this book includes a description of what you should be able to find in any program, method, or approach. You can choose the packaging and theme that best fits your situation, but, should you come across reading instruction that shows no evidence of the seven non-negotiables described in this book, you have found something atheoretical and dangerous. Drop it. Lives depend on your finding something else.

Identifying what's non-negotiable about high-quality reading instruction requires a working model of how people learn to read. In the following pages you will find an outline of one such model that will be used throughout the book.

It is important to point out from the beginning that this is one of many possible ways to conceptualize reading development, sources of difficulty, and the role of instruction. If you look at the titles of the hundreds of existing "how-to" books for reading instruction, you'll find that there's an ongoing debate about things as silly as whether or not "reading is rocket science."

Unfortunately, if high-quality reading instruction is constructed as a debate or a mystery rather than as a possibility for those who would teach it, reading will remain a mystery for too many students. Studies of exemplary reading teachers from across the country over the last sixty years have concluded that there is no one right way to teach reading.

However, if one takes a look at the number of students who struggle with reading, the percentage of special education referrals that list a reading-related difficulty as the reason for referral, and the number of incarcerated people with low literacy skills, there seem to be a lot of wrong ways to teach reading. Or, more to the point, there are a lot of things called reading instruction that are nothing of the sort.

So, those responsible for reading instruction have a right to a sense of clarity and empowerment in their work. If literacy is a human right, then you have a right to know about it. Figure 1 shows a model that outlines cycles of reading success and (in the opposite direction) cycles of reading difficulty. It is not perfect or all inclusive, but it does provide a useful way of thinking and talking about reading development, along with some of the possible snags and snafus that are common across ages and settings.

Figure 1 takes as its starting point the notion that reading is a self-extending process (Clay, 1991). That is, reading development depends, in part, on exposure to print and practice making sense of print; thus the act of reading fuels development. As Reading Hall of Famer Richard Allington famously says, "Kids teach themselves how to read with a little bit of help from their peers, and sometimes from their teachers" (personal communication).

One of the few things exemplary first- and fourth-grade reading teachers have in common is that they routinely use more of the allotted time for reading instruction to let students read. Less successful teachers routinely take the same allotted time and fill it with activities around and about reading

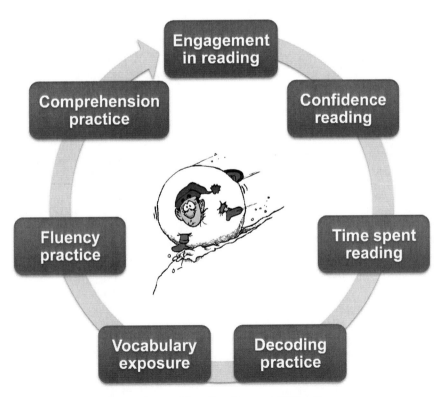

Figure 1.   The Snowball Cycle of Reading Success/Difficulty.

(worksheets, prereading activities, vocabulary games); so their students spend less time actually reading (Allington & Johnston, 2002).

Interestingly, less successful teachers are often a bit busier: designing and copying lots of "stuff" for kids to do, or giving instructions for long periods of time instead of simply allowing students to read or write during school. Exemplary teachers do teach, but they also know when to get out of the way and let a student's reading ability self-extend.

Reading development can happen in snowballing cycles of success or failure. No matter where you begin on the cycle, all factors feed one another in reciprocal relationships that could foster exponential growth.

For example, perhaps your first experiences with literacy made you interested in text and what it signifies, labels, or how it functions in stories or newspapers. Perhaps your interest led to time spent attending to print, noticing the patterns, and perhaps applying what you knew (or were learning) about sound-symbol correspondence (what sounds go with each letter). With a little instruction, time spent attending to print became time spent practicing the skill of recognizing words (decoding).

Since word recognition is a skill that requires some memory, some strategy, and some experience, time spent practicing decoding words increases your ability to decode. Time spent decoding more words also means you are exposed to more printed words and thus gives you the opportunity to be exposed to words you do not often hear in conversation (vocabulary).

Even small children reading simple texts will be exposed to words in text that they rarely, if ever, hear in conversation, which is partly why reading is one of the most efficient ways to increase vocabulary. Practice recognizing words and exposure to lots of words made it easier for you to read quickly and smoothly (fluency).

If and only if you can read quickly and smoothly enough to hold the words in mind to think about them together, you have a shot at comprehension. If and only if you comprehend what you are reading, then will you have a shot at liking it and feeling good about it (confidence), which could lead to engagement and perhaps motivation to attend to print at other times and in other settings.

This sense of motivation, combined with experiences of success, might inspire you to spend more time reading (engagement), which means more practice decoding, more vocabulary exposure, which means greater fluency, which means you have a shot at comprehension, which means you might like it more, which means you feel good about it, which means you spend time doing it, which means more practice, more exposure, more of a chance to understand, which means more of a chance to like it and more of a chance you'll continue to do it. Get the picture?

On the other hand, if there is a breakdown in any part of this cycle, the cycle can start snowballing the other direction with each component limiting the other in a cycle of reading difficulty. For example, perhaps you liked the idea of reading as a child, but struggled to make sense of decoding instruction in kindergarten. The time you spent attempting to decode printed words was fraught with frustration and failure, which simply meant you spent less time voluntarily doing it.

That does not mean you received less instruction or spent less time attempting to read in school (though failure and frustration might be reasons to avoid instruction through passivity or misbehavior). It may simply mean that you do not attend to the text that surrounds you in the environment.

When your siblings or classmates attended to the print on cereal boxes, street signs, store windows, and menus, racking up minute after minute of incidental practice every day, you looked away or around because you knew it was useless to try: the letters did not make sense.

Meanwhile, others were, with very little effort, increasing the amount of decoding practice and exposure to written words and speeding along through the cycle. High-success experiences with decoding made it so that opportunities to practice making meaning from printed language were perpetually available to them. While others became collectors of patterns, purposes, and possibilities for the written word in all its forms, you did not.

This breakdown could just have easily been at some other place in the cycle, but would have a similar effect. For example, you may have been a capable and engaged reader in school, but when you signed up for an advanced science class, you found that the texts were saturated with unknown vocabulary and organized in a way that did not make sense to you.

These challenges were both easily mediated by a science teacher who could explain the new words and unique features of the text. But you entered the interaction with this text having kinks in your reading cycle at vocabulary, comprehension, and therefore confidence and motivation, which made you less likely to feel good about reading or spend time doing it, and less likely to put in the additional practice.

This frustrating reading experience may not immediately or permanently damage your confidence or stunt your progress, but if it goes on unrepaired, you may begin to doubt your ability as a reader.

The image of a snowball cycle of reading success or difficulty also illustrates what is referred to as the "Matthew Effect" in reading (Stanovich, 1986). Stanovich named the pattern of relative success and failure in reading because it followed the pattern in the biblical story of Matthew in which "the rich get richer" (good readers become better and better) and the "poor get poorer" (reluctant or struggling readers struggle more and more as their difficulty compounds over time).

The Matthew Effect takes into account the affective and emotional aspects of reading (engagement, confidence, motivation), which both fuel and are fueled by successful reading experiences. Since reading is complex (many component skills), personal (we draw on prior knowledge and emotional resources), and necessary (for work, school, travel, relationships), high-success experiences are vital for the process to self-extend. That often means that a steady diet of easy texts is the fastest way to improve.

You can add medium and great challenges to this diet, but if you take away the high-success opportunities, progress can be stilted or reversed. Since people read and develop at different rates, this can present a challenge when learning is supposed to occur in group settings, as in classrooms.

In the chapters that follow, the non-negotiables described are designed to address this very challenge. Taken together, they facilitate each part of the cycle of reading success, are themselves supported by a deep research base, and will support you in designing, evaluating, and carrying out reading instruction that could make every child a reader.

Though we may each take different paths to literacy, these non-negotiables are a supportive frame for all of our efforts toward meaning making and should therefore be available in some measure for every reader, every day.

They are (in chapter order):

- Every reader reads something he or she chooses.
- Every reader reads accurately.
- Every reader reads something he or she understands.
- Every reading intervention is balanced to incorporate meaning.
- Every reader writes about something meaningful.
- Every reader talks with peers about reading and writing.
- Every reader listens to a fluent reader read aloud.

POINTS FOR DISCUSSION

1. Consider your own literacy history. Were there times that you struggled with reading or found yourself disliking it? Were some subjects easier than others to read? What component in the cycle might have propelled you forward or held you back at these times?
2. Which components of the cycle are explicitly addressed by your reading curriculum or with which approach are you most familiar?

Chapter One

Every Reader Reads Something He or She Chooses

The cycle of reading success described by the Matthew Effect (Stanovich, 1986) cannot begin or continue without the related elements of motivation and engagement. Since reading is an interaction between a reader and a text within a given context (Snow, 2002), giving a choice of texts allows readers to create the best possible interaction for the greatest possible level of engagement.

Remember, engagement leads to more time spent reading, which leads to better reading, better feelings about reading . . . and more reading! Choice is also motivating in and of itself because it provides a sense of agency and autonomy: both ingredients for motivation and self-determination.

WHY CHOICE IS NON-NEGOTIABLE

The evidence supporting the provision of choice as a regular part of reading instruction is both cohesive and definitive. It is supported by two areas of research that are very briefly highlighted here: research specific to reading motivation and research on human motivation in general.

Within the field of reading, Guthrie and Humenick's 2004 meta-analysis of twenty-two different studies of reading motivation concluded that the two factors that mattered most to both reading motivation and comprehension were (1) access to interesting texts and (2) personal choice of what to read.

Similarly, Ivey and Broaddus report that their 2001 survey of almost 2,000 sixth graders showed that choice of what to read, access to interesting choices, and being read to were the three most powerful factors in increasing the motivation to read. The impact of providing choice for adult learners can likewise not be underestimated given that autonomy and self-determination are the hallmarks of adult learning styles (Knowles, 1990).

Self-determination theory (Deci & Ryan, 1985), among other theories of motivation, provides a practical and compelling framework that describes why choice is fundamentally important to motivation, and motivation fundamentally important to learning.

Self-determination theory says that healthy development and functioning depends on three basic psychological needs: autonomy, competence, and relatedness. Deci and Ryan explain that

> Conditions supporting the individual's experience of *autonomy*, *competence*, and *relatedness* are argued to foster the most volitional and high quality forms of motivation and engagement for activities, including enhanced performance, persistence, and creativity. (Deci & Ryan, 2012)

This is true not just in schools or within educational pursuits, but across settings, such as in organizations, sport, religion, parenting, and relationships. Researchers who have investigated this theory have found that students with a sense of autonomy are more likely to value a task, feel positive about it, and experience engagement with it.

A teacher's role in supporting student autonomy breaks down into three areas:

- Providing choice
- Fostering relevance
- Allowing students to critique and evaluate tasks (rather than accepting them as they are)

All three of these autonomy-supporting strategies are engaged when students are allowed to choose what they read. For example, students are likely to choose texts that align with their interests and goals; thus choice leads to increased relevance.

The ability to choose invites evaluation of options; thus students are invited to think and act independently. Finally, the act of providing choice demonstrates some faith in the student, which supports the human need for a feeling of relatedness, automatically positioning them as *capable* of choosing and perhaps even *competent* to make a good choice.

The simple act of saying to a reader, "Which of these would you like to read?" can improve everything from the instructional interaction to the level of performance, persistence, and creativity the student brings to the reading task. Other theories of motivation—for example expectancy theory (Vroom, 1964)—similarly highlight the idea that the product of desire and confidence in your own ability is motivation, or action, or both ("I can x I want = I will").

We *can* do things we do not want to do or do not think we will do well. Still, given the importance of reading practice and engagement, the question should not be *can* we but *will* we. Will we attend to the texts that surround us? Will we use the allocated time for real, engaged reading? Will we choose to read in order to gain information, escape the day, be entertained, or learn?

These theories of motivation also serve as reminders that some aspects of a student's motivation to read are not accessible to us as instructors: they are deeply personal, situational, and invisible. But choice is always available to instructors as a tool to leverage student motivation as well as increase the likelihood of a successful reading experience.

THE PROS AND CONS OF CHOICE

Given all of the evidence for allowing readers to choose what they read, you may wonder why we ever tell readers what to read. You may wonder why, given the dangers of differential practice in school settings, we expect large groups of students to read the same text, for the same amount of time, and get the same benefit from it.

There are some real but surmountable challenges associated with offering readers a choice of what to read, especially in academic settings. These challenges are explored below with the goal of balancing, not dismissing, them in order to integrate choice for every reader, every day.

Coverage

In traditional school settings, reading, English, or language arts curricula are as much about teaching specific texts as they are about teaching reading. It is important to expose students to certain examples of literature and important to establish common texts so that classes can have discussions and shared experiences with meaning making.

Advocating for choice does not negate the need for common texts or exposure to grade-level literature—it complements it. In order for entire classes to understand and benefit from a common text, they must also have a steady diet of interesting and accessible texts to build their set of strategies and solidify their skills.

They must have banks of other texts with which to compare, and experiences with reading that have increased their confidence, interest, and sense of what Alfred Tatum (2009) calls a textual lineage. A textual lineage is a reader's sense of their lives in the context of the literature (or more broadly, the texts) that surrounds them: the stories that relate to their lives, the characters they admire, the ways of making meaning that resonate with them.

In his book about literacy instruction for African American males, Tatum wrote:

> It's not just about their literacy, it's about their lives. That's why no reading strategy, no literacy program, no remediation will close the achievement gap for adolescent African American males . . . That's why we will continue to fail our students, until reading instruction is anchored in meaningful texts that build academic and personal resiliency inside and outside school. (Tatum, 2005)

He argued that the texts we "cover" in school should be selected because they provide the ideas and motifs that can be used as raw materials for building a life, not because they are on the list or in the book room.

Though Tatum wrote about African American males specifically, the concept and importance of having a sense of textual lineage is not limited to this group. It is part of why any of us choose to read, and how we develop a sense of context and meaning for texts in our lives.

In math, the parallel concept would be number sense: the basic, almost intuitive understanding of numbers and how they work. We need to have experiences with a wide range of self-selected, readable texts in order to develop a sense of ourselves as readers and a sense of our lives in literature.

Since no teacher could ever find a series of one-size-fits-all texts—either in terms of content or level of difficulty—the use of choice reading provides a necessary balance for the inherent difficulties of forcing everyone to read the same thing. It leaves room for readers to practice their skills independently on their individual independent levels and provides a way to develop the background knowledge to read and appreciate texts they do not choose.

Teachers who are worried about covering required material should invest in choice because it makes "coverage" possible. Without some opportunity to choose what you read, the texts that are "covered"—those great books and classics—are more likely to be met by disengaged readers with little interest or confidence in the tasks chosen for them.

Teachers are also often worried that students would have little chance of success on standardized tests if they had never been exposed to certain texts that were at the level of difficulty aligned with their high-stakes assessment. These are both very real concerns, but neither are reasons to eliminate choice from the curriculum, let alone the school day.

As Kelly Gallagher (2009), English teacher and author, puts it: what students often need is a 50/50 split between grade-level texts and independent-level texts—that is, approximately half of the time reading or being exposed to (via read aloud or a shared or supported reading experience) the kinds of texts they will be held accountable for. This ensures students develop familiarity with and strategies for grade-level texts whether these are more or less difficult than those on their current independent reading level.

This 50/50 split requires a different set of resources than are often found in classrooms, especially at the secondary level. Instead of investing in many copies of a few texts, teachers might advocate ordering a few copies of many texts to be shared across classrooms. Since students can often read more challenging texts when they have interest and background for them, variety of options is as important as volume. (See "points for discussion" for more ideas about gathering texts).

In a 50/50 classroom, students who read above grade level get to spend half their time continuing to push themselves and half the time reading a common text that can be used for lessons and discussions. Thus this 50/50 split is a recipe for equal opportunities for challenge without giving up the benefit of shared reading experiences.

In order to rise to the level of too-hard texts, readers require supported exposure and time spent reading something they *can* read in order to solidify the skills and strategies they are developing. When it comes to text difficulty, the metaphor of weight lifting is often helpful to keep in mind.

For example, if the goal for the end of the year is to lift 100 pounds, but you can only lift 50, it would be dangerous and counterproductive to go to the gym every day to pull and pull and pull on that 100 pound barbell until you can get it off the ground. Instead, you would start at or slightly below the heaviest weight you can lift and put in the reps (practice) to build up to heavier bars.

As you prepare for the weightlifting competition, you would probably be sure to lift challenging weights with a spotter guiding your form and shouldering some of the excess weight. This ensures that you have some experience working at the highest level possible and are familiar with what it feels like to be faced with that 100-pound challenge.

If the required text is far above or below your current reading level, pulling endlessly isn't going to make it work. Instead, practice at your own level (whether above or below) and a guided approach to the target text (mediated by a teacher, peer or discussion) will ensure you develop as a reader and "cover" what you need to.

Materials

Choice is sometimes withheld because of the fear that there will not be enough to choose from. In settings where there are limited texts available, it is important to keep in mind that *controlled* choice is better than no choice at all. That is, having the choice of only two or three options is still preferable than being assigned a task with no say in it.

In situations where the text cannot be changed or substituted, choice can be incorporated in other aspects of the reading experience including where students are allowed to sit, what they do while they read or after they read, and whether they read alone or with a peer.

The layer of choice does not *have* to include choice of text, but when it does, students are more likely to select something that aligns with their goals and interests and is thus powered by their intrinsic motivation. One only has to look at the shelves of magazines that line bookstores, and even some grocery stores, to see how powerfully our interests and hobbies guide our reading (and purchasing) choices.

Though an interest in basketball doesn't automatically mean you like to read about basketball, the background/subject-specific knowledge our hobbies provide are invaluable to comprehension (Guthrie, Wigfield, Metsala, & Cox, K., 1999; Baldwin, Peleg-Bruckner & McClintock, 1985).

In fact, middle school students who choose leisure reading materials based on their hobbies and areas of interests are able to understand texts that are leveled several years above their grade level because of the boost that their interest and prior knowledge provide (Gabriel, Allington, & Billen, 2012). This is also why series books that build on the plot or structure of one another are such powerful supports for struggling or reluctant readers (McGill-Franzen, 2010). The "special powers" of series books will be explored in chapter 2.

If students select something they do not enjoy, their role as the "chooser" positions them as being capable of critiquing the text. Acting as a text critic can be interesting in and of itself. And, if students can support their critique, they can choose to abandon a text they do not enjoy without abandoning the opportunity to learn from it.

Maturity and Fit

Adults often worry that inexperienced readers, or even sometimes experienced readers, will choose texts that are a bad fit either in terms of appropriate content or level of difficulty. If the content of available texts is a concern, providing a limited choice (choose from this set of teacher- or parent-selected options) rather than the world of texts, will still have the desired impact.

In school settings this often takes the form of a "browsing box" or a system of leveling and sorting texts by topic and difficulty to facilitate efficient and meaningful choices. Teachers should also be assured that there is mounting evidence that readers are likely to try to find texts that they can and want to read. Given the choice, students make good ones, even if they sometimes surprise us.

The same way no one makes a habit of reading in a language they don't understand simply because they can sound out the words, few people voluntarily choose texts that are too difficult for them to read. When they do, it is often for a social reason (wanting to look like a good reader, wanting to blend in), which can be addressed by masking reading choices (as with book covers or electronic readers that don't make the title of the text obvious to observers), or describing connections between desired texts and related, but easier possibilities.

If you feel the need to challenge a reader's choice, realize that you are not just challenging the text, but their very autonomy and ability to choose for themselves. In order to ensure your veto power is used wisely, you might follow a three-step challenge process:

1. Allow students the opportunity to keep their chosen text by demonstrating that they can and want to read it. You may be surprised how well students tackle difficult texts when they are motivated and have the background knowledge to understand them.
2. Ask students to tell you why they chose the text so that you can apply this rationale to future options or recommendations.
3. Never say never. With a too-hard text that a student is interested in, it's never "goodbye"; it's only "see you later." Send the message that "*when* this text is a good fit for you (which I have faith it will be one day) it will be waiting for you . . . Moreover, I will be here to congratulate you." But, knowing the importance of matching readers to texts they can read, you might say, "For now, based on your own rationale for this choice I suggest a few alternatives." With a too-easy text, especially a favorite that has been read over and over again, it is likewise never "goodbye," but "see you when I have earned a break from challenge," or "when I want to share my reading skills with a younger reader."

Choosing a text can be an expression of a reader identity, so teachers should be careful when assuming they know better than the reader what should be read. For example, in our study of the magazine-reading habits of middle school students (Gabriel, Allington, & Billen, 2012), we found that students often choose magazines that readability formulas and leveling systems would deem too difficult for them. But, when we asked students to read these magazines aloud and talk about what they'd read, we found that they were capable of reading and understanding texts far above their tested level (see table 1.1).

In a study of *Full On* magazine, a text that was made freely available to adolescents in the UK, students reported that it was also easier to be seen with a magazine than a book because of the assumptions peers make about those who walk around with books in hand (Carnell, 2005). In the United States, magazines are among the top ten items adolescents will purchase with their own money, right up there with candy, snacks, and music. Books, however, are not on the list (Magazine Publishers of America, 2004).

Table 1.1.   Magazine Choices by Reading Level

Magazine title	Number of times selected	Topic	Estimated range of grade-level equivalents*	Students who chose this title but read below its range of levels
Twist	19	Lifestyle	2nd–7th grade	0/19
Tiger Beat	12	Lifestyle	2nd–7th grade	0/12
North American Whitetail	11	Hunting	5th–12th grade	8/11
Gamepro	14	Video games	6th–12th grade	10/14
PC Gamer	10	Computer games	6th–12th grade	5/10
Dirt Rider	8	Outdoor sports	5th–12th grade	4/8
J-14	15	Lifestyle	2nd–11thgrade	0/15
Seventeen	8	Lifestyle	3rd–11th grade	0/8

*Given that no readability or leveling system is specifically designed for use with magazine texts, levels were calculated using the lowest and highest levels generated by either of two readability formulas and one qualitative leveling rubric in order to present the widest possible range.
Source: Gabriel, Allington & Billen, 2012. Used with permission.

A close look at many magazines, especially special interest magazines, demonstrates that they contain a bank of texts of varying structures and genres as well as varying difficulty. Magazines are a good example of a practical option for those who want to appear to be reading something harder than they are currently capable of: they contain a range of texts with supportive text features (pictures, captions, etc.) all on the same general subject. They are also a good reminder that many things besides books should be allowed to count as real reading because they contain the important elements despite their alternative formats.

A text is a text if it requires readers to make meaning from sets of symbols, usually and especially printed words, with recognizable formatting and organizational features. That means sign posts, cereal boxes, websites, warning labels, and baseball cards have to be allowed to count, if for no other reason than that they matter to people. They are practical examples of texts someone might use and value in their everyday lives. That is more than can be said for plenty of books, so they should count for choice reading.

What If They Choose Nothing?

We often have to be taught what there is to like or appreciate about texts before it occurs to us to like or appreciate them. Like listening to the radio in a car where the driver has commandeered the tuner, we have to be able to find *something* to appreciate in everything—even if it's only appreciating how cutting and erudite our critique can be.

With music, it could be the rhythm, the melody, the pace, the words, the fact that it's over quickly . . . because we are often surrounded (and bombarded) by it, we can find a range of different aspects to enjoy without actually loving the song. Likewise with texts, especially academic texts, it helps to know what there is to like about them. Is it like something I've read before? Does it give me information I can't get anywhere else? Is it funny? Poetic? Historic? Should it remind me of something? An important question to answer within any recommendation for a text is: What is there to like about it?

At the very least, readers are more likely to find something enjoyable about texts they can easily understand. For the purpose of efficient choosing, the "five-finger" or "Goldilocks principle" comes in handy for choosing a "just right" book. This rule directs readers to count on their fingers how many words out of a page they don't know.

If they read and count to five fingers on one hand, it's too hard. If no fingers are used, it is likely to be so easy that they won't be exposed to new words. If it's between zero and five fingers, they are likely to understand enough of the text to infer the meaning of the few unfamiliar words, and thus, begin to learn them through exposure.

This guideline is less useful for beginning readers who may only find a few words per page (five unknown words could be literally half of the book). In this case it may make sense for early readers to choose based on interest rather than level, and to limit choices to a controlled set of options in which students are likely to find something they can and want to read.

Like Goldilocks, we are always looking for something that's not too easy, not too hard, but "just right." Though this may sound elementary, it is perhaps most useful in the middle grades when a wide range of texts hold interest and "appropriate" content, but come in the widest range of difficulty.

Presenting this as a "five-finger rule" (rather than the Goldilocks principle) may make this important and efficient strategy more appealing to older readers. Likewise, an explanation of the impact of time spent reading something you can and want to read (see table 1.2) can provide older readers with the context for embracing this simple tool as their own.

Table 1.2 has been spotted on the walls of classrooms for students of all ages in a variety of settings. It has served as a truly inspirational reminder that practice pays off and that time spent reading matters. It can also serve as a warning and advertisement for the importance of ensuring readers have learned how to find texts they can read and want to read.

The first thing you might notice about this chart is that there is a clear correlation between time spent reading and reading achievement. Specifically, there is exponential growth in exposure (words per year) based on small increases in minutes of reading per day. In order to "read" more of the stories this chart has to tell, and there are many, it's important to know where it came from.

This data comes from a study of the self-reported out-of-school reading habits of 156 fifth graders (Anderson, Wilson, & Fielding, 1988). Students in the study kept reading diaries for several months and were given a fluency test that measured their average words read per minute. Researchers multiplied students' average time spent reading out of school with their individual average words read per minute (wpm) and found these averages correlated with achievement on standardized reading tests. This is the evidence most often cited to support the idea that time spent reading equals reading success.

The fact that it was generated using self-reported out-of-school reading is even more compelling because it means that more than minutes went into this striking correlation. Students did not go into a controlled, laboratory environment where some read more than others in order to prove that exposure to print alone led to greater achievement. This is minutes per day beyond the school day.

The numbers above included time spent reading homework, outside academic work, and leisure reading. Students who read the least, either didn't have homework, didn't do their homework, or didn't view their homework as actual reading. It is easier to imagine that the minutes represent actual time spent reading, rather than allocated time for reading since the data is self-reported.

The table also tells several other stories. For example, unlike practicing the piano, becoming expert at reading doesn't require that you practice six hours a day. In fact, small differences in time spent reading translate to large differences in exposure and outcomes.

Table 1.2.   Variation in Amount of Independent Reading

Achievement percentile	Minutes of reading per day	Words per year
90th	40.4	2,357,000
50th	12.9	601,000
10th	1.6	51,000

Source: Anderson, Wilson, & Fielding, 1988. Used with permission.

Even at the 90th percentile, reading doesn't require hours of practice and engagement. In fact, it seems to require less than an hour outside of school. And, every minute counts.

WHAT YOU SHOULD SEE IN A CLASSROOM WITH CHOICE

Students will be reading. When you ask what they're reading, they will tell you what it is and why they chose it. They will tell you if they like it and what it tells them about future reading choices they might make. Providing choice not only ensures opportunities for successful engagement now, but invests in future successful reading experiences.

In summary, there are two primary reasons to invest in the practice of providing readers with some choice about what they read. First, they are likely to choose texts that will allow them to have a high-success reading experience, which is necessary for a cycle of reading success. Second, it is likely to provide readers with a sense of independence and agency, both of which will positively contribute to their motivation to read.

A classroom that has invested in the power of choice has a variety of options on a range of levels. This does not have to mean every classroom needs it's own extensive library; if infrastructure and resources limit class-room libraries, there needs to be a comprehensive system of rotating books between classrooms, or a partnership with an agency (online or in person) that can provide access to more texts. Below are some specific suggestions for accomplishing this.

FOUR POWERFUL AND MANAGEABLE WAYS TO INVEST IN CHOICE

1. Invest in efficient ways to ensure readers have access to a wide range of texts they find interesting.

This includes electronic resources that provide access to a bank or library of texts; periodicals that ensure the regular delivery of new and possibly timely texts, such as magazines and newspapers; subscription series or book clubs that likewise provide a steady stream of materials at a discounted rate; and, finally, free texts like brochures, manuals, fact sheets, flyers, and informa-tional booklets that are so often available from public agencies, but over-looked because they are short or nonacademic. These very features could be the exact reason a reader is interested in them: they are practical, informa-tional, and brief, often with supportive visuals or other text features, connec-tions to life experiences or interests, and little challenge to stamina.

2. Ensure a balance between ease and challenge in order to ensure the solidification of skills and a reassuring speed of progress.

High-success reading experiences are invaluable to the cycle of reading success. Still, challenging texts surround developing or struggling readers, sometimes on a daily or even hourly basis. They need strategies to attack too-hard texts as well as time to rise to the level where there are fewer to contend with. They also need models of what it should look like to do the complex and demanding work of understanding a too-hard text. This is the topic further addressed in chapter 3.

3. Stretch your imagination to increase the range and volume of texts you can offer to your readers.

There are a surprising number of sources for free texts as well as several ways to share and rotate collections that may already exist in your building.

Ways to take advantage of free reading material:

- Educator memberships at public libraries often allow you to take out more texts for longer periods of time. Librarians may even assist you in creating a set of books around a certain topic or level of difficulty that you can take out for a time, and then swap out for a new set after several weeks. This creates a rotating shelf of new options at literally no cost.
- Arrange a book swap in your school or community. Let readers earn a credit for every book they bring in, and let them choose a book for every credit they earn. If people mostly turn in books that are far above or below the level of your readers, consider involving a local school or library that might widen the collection and offer a good home to books your readers don't choose.
- Begin a habit of picking up free brochures and other literature from stores, offices, and agencies. ASPCA pet care pamphlets and free driver manuals are particular hits in middle school libraries.
- Bookmark or print online documents that match a particular interest (profiles of sports teams, biographies, product reviews, etc.).
- Allow current and former students to enter their own writing into the collection available for independent reading. This not only honors their work, it ensures a steady supply of texts written by and for a group of peers.

Ways to maximize the use of texts in your building:

- Organize book talks given by colleagues, outside speakers, or members of the class to highlight the books in your collection and give readers ideas of what they might read next. This also provides exposure to literate conversations and role models for reading.

- Have readers write recommendations or give oral presentations that advertise texts they've enjoyed. Keeping a list of what students will read next based on recommendations ensures they spend less time trying to choose and more time looking forward to reading.
- Create a "sisterhood of the traveling book bin" between teachers or create a pushcart that can house a small collection of books that can be shared between classrooms. This way forty books per classroom can turn into 120 books for a team of three classrooms. Readers can write and read recommendations for their peers in other classes.
- Invest in periodicals or book clubs that continue to send fresh, new material throughout the year for one flat cost.
- Order with interests in mind. When in doubt, order a series (see chapter 2 for the research on reading series books, and appendix C for ways to identify series books by topic or difficulty).

4. Fund expansions of reading options by eliminating all the materials in your budget that do not have empirical proof of their impact on reading motivation or achievement.

- Though many of the strategies above can be implemented at low or no cost, access to lots of texts costs money. And it adds value to a reader's experience. Ruthlessly cut out budget items that are not proven to add value, and invest in those that are.
- These unproven materials include workbooks, copy paper for worksheets, and most computer tutorial programs.

Note: Abandoning workbooks and worksheets can spark resistance and cause a great deal of anxiety for those who have relied on them, at worst, to manage behavior by keeping students busy, and at best, to reinforce skills. Moreover, schools and districts have invested millions of dollars in these tools and often loathe throwing them away. The suggestion here is to keep them as resources, but defund future purchases of such materials.

Convincing teachers and administrators to abandon materials they have always used may require a gradual approach (teachers need time to develop strategies and systems for all the time that used to be spent on worksheets) and a clear presentation of the rationale for the change.

Appendix A is a protocol for guiding an analysis of the relative value of a reading-related assignment, specifically a worksheet. If applied to examples used in your school setting it should spark conversations about the aspects of a worksheet that hold value for readers (there aren't many) and those that don't. It ends with a set of questions that are designed to guide a conversation about the kinds of activities your staff wants to engage in and where such materials do or do not fit in.

If you find a worksheet or style of assignment that matches your vision for excellent reading instruction, by all means invest in it. If instead you find that the materials are moderately supportive, but mostly mindless, use this to form a shared understanding of the need for change.

POINTS FOR DISCUSSION

- What sorts of texts are favorites among the readers you work with? Why do you think this is? What is similar about these texts and the text you currently invest in?
- Where do most of the texts come from in your school? What other sources of texts could you use?

Chapter Two

Every Reader Reads Accurately

Reading accurately solidifies decoding strategies by rewarding the reader's efforts with text that makes sense. It also fuels cycles of reading success by feeding accurately recognized words into meaning-making processes.

A classroom where students have the opportunity to read accurately may not always provide independent-level texts to all students, but every student will have at least one regularly scheduled opportunity during the day to read something they *can* read accurately. It doesn't have to be all the time, but it can't be never. In fact, only a few minutes a few days a week will add up to a large amount of high-success (accurate) practice over the year.

Table 2.1 illustrates how a few minutes every day or each week can add up to large amounts of reading practice as well as opportunities for teachers to work with students individually. Making time for independent reading doesn't necessarily require an infusion of additional time or funding, just a reallocation of small, but regular, amounts of time over the year.

In the upper grades, multiply these figures by the number of content area teachers who also allow, model, and encourage reading. If you are faithfully providing choice and access to interesting texts, this small investment of time could just balloon out into large amounts of voluntary reading during out-of-school leisure time.

WHY ACCURACY IS NON-NEGOTIABLE

Accuracy is non-negotiable because it mediates the possibility of comprehension and reinforces decoding skill. If students never or rarely have the opportunity to read something they can read with accuracy they implicitly learn that their word attack or decoding strategies don't work and that reading either doesn't make sense or always has to be hard.

Table 2.1.   Accumulation of Allocated Time for Reading

Option	Time spent reading	Positives	Time over a month	Time over a year	One-to-one time*
Fridays, end of the day/period	15–20 min, 1x a week	Doesn't require reorganizing current instructional time, uses "dead"/ transition time	60–80 min	9–12 hours	2–4x
Fridays and Mondays end/ beginning of day	15–20 min, 2x a week		120–160 min	18–24 hours	5–8x
Every other day	15–25 min	Part of instructional routine. Gives you time to conference with every student	135–200 min	20–30 hours	6–9x
Daily	15–25 min		300–500 min	45–75 hours	13–15x

*Conservative estimate of times the teacher could have a 5–10 minute individual conference with each student in a class of twenty.

This is why struggling readers will often read to the bottom of a page and turn it without understanding it: Without lots of practice reading accurately, they may not notice when text doesn't make sense. Some students are so used to text not making sense that it seems no different to them.

Strong readers do the exact opposite. They don't just read down a page and turn it, they stop at funny bits, reread interesting parts, notice when they've "spaced out" for a moment and go back to pick up the thread of meaning they have been spinning as they read. They recognize that text is supposed to make sense, and they use strategies to make meaning out of it when it doesn't.

When we take a close look at the component skills that are implicated in reading difficulty, the role of accurate reading comes into sharp relief. For example, in 2002, Florida passed a law that required all students who failed the state reading test in third grade to be retained. When people found that many children were retained not once, but multiple times as a result of this law, some started to question why another year of instruction wasn't making an impact on reading achievement.

In 2004, Sheila Valencia and Marsha Riddle-Buly investigated this phenomenon with a group of more than 100 fifth graders who had failed their state reading tests. The researchers delivered a battery of in-depth reading assessments to this large group in order find out specifically why they struggled.

They used a statistical procedure called cluster analysis to identify patterns in performance across the group and came up with six distinct profiles of struggling readers with different sets of strengths and needs. They concluded that providing the same intervention to readers who struggled for different reasons was a surefire way to ensure no one got just what they needed, and most got a whole lot less.

Table 2.2 describes the profiles they identified among readers who struggled. Interestingly, 67 percent of students (across four reader profiles) struggled with fluency. Fifty-nine percent struggled with meaning making, and 41 percent struggled with word identification (decoding). In other words, accuracy was a contributing factor for nearly half of students who failed the state test. A mere 9 percent struggled in all three areas. Note that the row label "disabled" does not mean 9 percent were diagnosed with a disability. The table simply uses this term for those that had difficulty across the three areas. "EL" refers to the percent of students in this category who were classified as English language learners.

Though accuracy is directly captured by the category of word identification, if words are identified incorrectly they will have an adverse impact on both decoding and fluency. Thus accurate reading underlies each of these areas of potential strength or difficulty.

In 2009, Danielle Dennis replicated this study with nearly 100 middle school students who had failed a state reading test in a different part of the country. She similarly found that there were identifiable profiles of readers within this group including: Strategic readers (slow, but meaning makers) slow word callers (so slow they struggled to make meaning), automatic word callers (accurate, but struggled to make meaning), and rapid readers (so quick they struggled to make meaning).

Table 2.2. Reader Profiles

Reader profiles (% per sample)	Word Identification	Comprehension	Fluency	%EL
Automatic word callers (18%)	++	-	++	63%
Struggling word callers (15%)	-	-	++	56%
Word stumblers (17%)	-	+	-	16%
Slow comprehenders (24%)	+	++	-	19%
Slow word callers (17%)	+	-	-	56%
Disabled readers (9%)	--	--	--	20%

++Above average; +average; -below average; --substantially below average
Source: Valencia, 2011. Used with permission.

All three researchers concluded that a one-size-fits-all intervention could never meet the needs of students who had such different profiles of strengths and difficulties. Unfortunately for such children, ideology has trumped evidence: five more states have enacted automatic retention policies based on third grade reading scores and none of these policies mandates substantial, individualized differentiation for those who are retained.

One notable aspect of findings from this pair of studies is that a full 19 percent of elementary students and 8 percent of middle school students could read accurately with some comprehension, but failed simply because they didn't have the fluency (or stamina) to read test passages efficiently within the allotted time.

Of those who struggled with meaning making, more than half also struggled with fluency, which suggests that there is a strong link between the ability to read quickly and smoothly and the ability to understand what you read, especially during a timed assessment. Though fluency is not a prerequisite for comprehension, it is perhaps its strongest facilitator.

IF ACCURACY MATTERS, DOES TEXT LEVEL?

In books published as early as 1946, Emmett Betts wrote about the need to differentiate literacy experiences for different readers. One of the central concepts he explored in the 1950s was the idea of identifying the optimal text difficulty an individual required for learning. Similar to the Vygotskian notion of a zone of proximal development, Betts argued that matching readers with texts they could read and learn from was an important part of literacy instruction.

In fact, it was one of his doctoral students who came up with the idea of independent (95–100 percent accuracy), instructional (90–95 percent accuracy), and frustration (< 90 percent accuracy) levels. Yet, as another reading researcher, Tim Shanahan (2011), pointed out, there is surprisingly little evidence for the theory that a text's assigned level should specifically match a reader's tested ability, in part because text difficulty is relative.

For example, a ten-word math problem requires nearly 100 percent accuracy for understanding, whereas it is often quite possible to miss two or three words out of 150 in a descriptive narrative passage and still understand it.

As Chall and colleagues (1999) found in their qualitative analysis of text difficulty, one of the things that marks mounting difficulty in science textbooks is the density of information within each sentence. The density of information has an impact on the level of accuracy required to make meaning.

Consider the following sentences:

1. "The frog can swim in the water."
2. "It is possible to calculate that, if a frog oocyte (a developing egg cell) had the same number of ribosomal RNA genes as a body cell of the frog, it would take many years—far longer than a female frog lives— to make an egg with so many ribosomes." (Examples taken from Chall et al., 1999, pp. 29, 32)

These two sentences are taken from science textbooks that are ten grades apart. Though the sentences in science textbooks may get longer or more complex over time, Chall and colleagues suggest that changes in assumed background knowledge, specialized vocabulary, and the level of reasoning required should not be overlooked when estimating text difficulty. This means that individual students will find it relatively easier or harder based on their level of motivation and background knowledge, not necessarily their ability. With specialized texts, background knowledge and purpose for reading may be even more important to meaning making than accuracy.

Text difficulty is relative because comprehension is the product of an interaction between a reader, text, and activity. The idea that we could determine a reader's level and match it with a leveled text makes sense in theory, but is not perfect in practice. As Shanahan pointed out, any leveling or readability system, no matter how sophisticated or widely used, is only ever a general estimate. Factors within the reader (e.g., interest, background knowledge, confidence) as well as in the context (e.g., distractions, test format, text format) have an impact on the relative difficulty a reader will have with a given text.

Likewise, most attempts to identify an individual student's reading level are also relative estimates, not narrow or static diagnoses. When you put two guesstimates together, you should take the resulting assumptions with a huge hunk of salt. As we discussed in chapter 1, the expert on the match between a reader and a text is often the reader. If we want a good match between a reader and a text, we should support readers to choose texts they feel that they can read and want to read. Levels may help guide that choice, but they should not limit it.

We simply have too much evidence that motivation, interest, background knowledge and confidence influence reading success to limit students to texts of one readability level. Donalyn Miller, also known as the "Book Whisperer," says, "Looking at a child's face or a book's cover, I see possibility, not a number" (2012). She publically warns against overreliance on readability systems for matching readers to texts arguing that "slavish devotion to numbers doesn't benefit readers" (Miller, 2012).

Readability and leveling systems can be useful as guides, but it may be more helpful to use them to indicate the range of levels that might be appropriate for a reader rather than a specific or exclusive level.

INCREASING ACCURATE READING

Increasing the volume of accurate reading can be addressed by developing the skill of fluency. In order to compare various ways to increase accurate reading via fluency, it is worth exploring some of the uses and abuses of fluency instruction.

Fluency is defined by four interrelated factors—speed, accuracy, prosody (expression), and understanding—but is too often taught with a laser-like focus on either one (speed) or two factors (speed and accuracy). This has resulted in entire classrooms of students who are implicitly taught that reading means quickly calling out words as a conditioned response to a text stimulus.

If instruction focuses too closely on speed and accuracy, students are taught to value reciting instead of reading and pronouncing instead of understanding. If that sounds melodramatic, look at some of the assessments most commonly used to identify children in need of remediation or special education referrals (e.g., DIBELS) and calculate for yourself how much of a student's reading future is determined by the number of words they can "read" per minute.

Students are labeled as "struggling," "striving," or still "developing" on a regular basis because of the speed at which they read (or more specifically, the number of words they recite from a page when being timed for 60 seconds). Unfortunately for them, reading rate is an imperfect (and often inaccurate) measure of overall reading ability, in part because there is a ceiling on the rate at which it is reasonable to read.

As Scott Paris (2005) notes, "Data are highly variable and unstable over time for constrained skills like fluency. They are usually and necessarily skewed during initial acquisition and later mastery with variance that ranges from nil to large to nil during mastery" (p. 187). He argues that the skill of fluency has conceptual, developmental and methodological constraints that may cause changing and unstable relationships with other reading skills like comprehension.

The point of reading quickly and smoothly is to increase the chance that you will remember the beginning of the written thought by the time you've read the end of it. Speed is not an end in itself. Reading a mile-a-minute-like-the-micro-machine-man is no more strategic than reading as-slow-as-a-tortoise. In fact, slowing down your reading rate is sometimes the most effective strategy for repairing comprehension.

It isn't speed that matters; it's optimum processing volume: You need enough information in enough time for your brain to be able to put it together and process it at once—not too fast and not too slow.

For the most part, we are all striving for the spirit of a tempo musicians call *andante*: a walking speed, or, more specifically, the speed of normal, everyday conversation. Interestingly, musicians describe andante as about 76–108 beats per minute on a metronome. Hasbrouk and Tindall (2006) investigated the norms for fluency across elementary school grades. According to their normed reference scale, 76–108 words per minute is around the average fluency of an elementary school reader between third and fifth grade.

The danger of a metaphor that uses a tempo marking is that some people will start following students around with metronomes, or worse, stopwatches, and telling them that they have to read at 108 words per minute or they aren't good readers. The point of *andante* isn't the literal number, but the natural rhythm we find ourselves in when something has become so automatic that it doesn't require attentional resources.

The goal of fluency is likewise not a number, but the state of automaticity at whatever speed is most efficient for the mind it's meant to serve. Incidentally, this number associated with automatic reading will and should vary with the type of text, familiarity of the content and the context in which it's being read.

It's important to keep in mind that the goal is always optimal understanding, not optimal speed. Thus fluency programs or assessments that focus on speed and/or accuracy to the exclusion of (or in the absence of) meaning and understanding, are not only misleading, but miseducative.

Students can be taught to read much faster than the speed of conversation, sometimes even with prosody that implies meaning and responsiveness to punctuation, but it should not count as fluent reading if understanding is lost. Period.

Contrasting Approaches to Fluency Development

It is at the intersection of automaticity and meaning that scholars with divergent recommendations for fluency instruction meet. Everyone agrees that fluency should ultimately facilitate meaning making. Scholars diverge in their pathways towards this common goal of facilitative fluency.

On one end of the spectrum scholars advocate repeated reading of controlled texts. On the other, scholars advocate wide reading of a variety of texts. Scholars on the repeated reading end believe readers build fluency in layers by reading passages over and over again until they can be read quickly and smoothly, then moving on to a slightly harder passage and commencing this repetitive, drill-style practice again.

Though the mechanics of speed, accuracy and prosody can be improved with deliberate practice, the goal of reading for meaning may be thwarted by assignments and activities that require mind-numbing repetition of often meaningless passages for no other purpose than speed. Though there is some evidence that fluency on an individual passage transfers to new texts, the transfer is always only partial, as familiarity plays a role in fluency.

Scholars that advocate repeated reading accuse those who advocate wide reading of embracing mediocrity by allowing readers to read lots of texts with moderate accuracy without practicing each one until they read it well (Rasinski, 2010). They argue that this reinforces inadequate accuracy in the name of novelty.

The wide reading camp argues that exposure to a wide variety of texts develops strategies and comprehension problem-solving skills as well as increasing the possibility that readers have engaged with high-success, interesting reading experiences. They argue that wide exposure creates flexibility in strategy use and that practice of all kinds will surely add up. The benefit of this approach is exposure and the opportunity to find and enjoy texts, rather than being constrained to the repeated reading of contrived passages.

The marriage of these perspectives, the one that recognizes the need to read widely and the benefit of constrained practice, can often be found in performative approaches. That is, reader's theater, scripts for plays, reels for newscasts, lines for daily announcements, performances, and so forth. These provide reasons to read repeatedly, but for a purpose.

Rehearsal for performances provide the rare excuse to read the same thing over and over again without feeling as though you're hitting your head against a "Great Wall of Boring." In fact, the repetition is essential for memorization and/or performance for multiple audiences. Performance thus provides the best of both words: *repeated reading* for an *authentic purpose* that provides a pathway to engagement with a text.

As Rasinksi (2004) notes, performances do not require much in the way of time, materials, props, or scenery. They can be as elaborate as a play for the public or as simple as having students repeat the most important phrases of a text ("this time with feeling!") or a daily quote to each other in their boomiest announcer (or other) voices.

Some texts, like song lyrics and poems, have the repetition literally built in. Some episodic texts, like articles in a news series or books in a trilogy, provide similar support and practice towards expertise without verbatim repetition. This is especially true of series books.

THE SPECIAL POWERS OF SERIES BOOKS

Series books are prominent features on the International Reading Association's children's book awards list as well as the *New York Times* bestseller list. They are also perhaps most likely to be made into feature films and generate other spinoff features (TV, movies, plays, fan fiction). This is because we love them. And we love them, in part, because they become familiar.

As Anne McGill-Franzen (2010) has described, books in a series are supportive of struggling and reluctant readers because their internal structures are inherently repetitive. We can get hooked by the books and caught up in the social and media frenzy around reading them. Like the next episode of a favorite TV show, the release of a new installment carries a sense of excitement beyond that of a new single volume.

Cliffhangers and previews create anticipation and curiosity (motivation) for reading. Series books also create background knowledge that can make meaning making and context-building easier. For example, if you'd heard about *Harry Potter* from a friend, or seen clips of the movie before reading it, you would already know that "Hermione" sounds like "her-my-oh-knee." When you see it in print, instead of possibly getting stuck, you may make up your own pronunciation or already know which character it refers to.

Subsequent books in a series build off of the same character and settings names, sets of specialized vocabulary, and general plot structure, thus freeing up the reader to enjoy, rather than concentrate hard on meaning making. Once you've read book 1 of the Boxcar Children series, you know the names Henry, Jessie, Violet, Benny, and Watch. You know that Jessie is a girl, Benny is the youngest, Violet is a person, not a color, and Watch is a dog, not an accessory.

You also know what a boxcar is and why these four children have adventures that are largely independent of adults. You can sit back and enjoy the story. This combination of social supports for reading, generative background knowledge from other representations or overheard discussions of the text, and the broad repetition of characters, terms and themes ensure series books add fuel to every component of a cycle of reading success.

While series books may not lend themselves to every course's content focus, they are a reliable strategy for getting readers, even reluctant readers, hooked on something that could extend into leisure time and provide a high-success experience.

They also highlight aspects of texts teachers should capitalize on whether the book is in a series or not, including:

1. The novelty factor in excitement to read.
2. The social nature of reading and the support of familiarity and background knowledge.
3. The power of the media to shape what counts as current and interesting.

The combination of these aspects in series books is what makes them appear to have as many "special powers" about them as their characters have within them.

WHAT YOU SHOULD SEE IN A CLASSROOM WHERE EVERY READER READS ACCURATELY

1. There is a range of levels and types of texts to choose from for independent reading.
2. There is a regularly scheduled time for students to read.
3. When asked, students can explain what they're reading, why they chose it, and what they like best about it.
4. There are regular opportunities to reread texts for a specific purpose (performance, reading to younger peers, etc.).

POINTS FOR DISCUSSION

1. What subject-specific factors have you encountered that make understanding a text more or less difficult for students?
2. What are some of the ways teachers can address or mediate these potential sources of difficulty?
3. It is possible that familiarity with the genre and rich background knowledge make it easier for students to infer meaning even if they misidentify some individual words. What other factors or strategies might help someone comprehend a text in the absence of high levels of accuracy?

Chapter Three

Every Reader Reads Something He or She Understands

Time to read and access to texts are factors that could be referred to as "necessary, but not sufficient" (McGill-Franzen et al., 1999) for reading improvement. High-success reading experiences in which students *understand* what they read (and therefore engage, enjoy, build confidence, interest and want to read more), is a necessary, but too often ignored, mediator of reading success.

WHY UNDERSTANDING IS NON-NEGOTIABLE

Without a focus on meaning, reading is stripped of its empowering qualities. For example, in table 3.1., compare the teacher-student exchanges in word recognition-related activities that are routinely completed before reading a shared text.

Both of these short extracts are representative of commonly used programs that are considered "research-based," explicit instruction in the code system of English (e.g., phonics instruction or word study). Example 1 privileges the performance of word recognition as an automatic skill unto itself while example 2 privileges the process of word recognition as a strategy for decoding and encoding (reading and writing) even for words beyond those planned by a publisher for this lesson.

Example 1 uses a skill-drill approach with plenty of repetition, auditory and visual input, and routines to support participation. Students are asked to read for speed and accuracy, and to spell accurately and automatically from memory. Words are not linked to their meaning(s) or read for understanding.

Table 3.1. Examples Transcribed from Publicly Available YouTube Videos of First Grade Reading Instruction

Example 1: *Students all respond in unison at the cue of a teacher's snapped fingers.*	Example 2: *Students respond individually by raising their hands.*
T: Word 1. What word? (snap) Ss: Sliced T: Spell it (snap) Ss: S-l-i-c-e-d T: Word 2. What word? (snap) Ss: Cliff T: Spell it (snap) Ss. C-l-i-f-f T: Let's read those words again the fast way, all of them. Get ready (snap) Ss: Sliced, cliff. http://www.youtube.com/watch?v= 3cwODCQ9BnU&feature=related	T: Ok let's go back to the gl- blend. Who can tell me a word that begins with the gl- sound? S: Gladiator T: Ooh that's a really long one. What do you hear at the beginning of gladiator? What word, do you hear a word at the beginning of it? S: Glad T: Glad. Good. Let's do that one because it's short and I think we can do that one. Let's do glad. (Students begin to write on individual whiteboards.) Who knows what short vowel sound "glad" has in it that we've been talking about? S: Oh, it's "a" T: That short "a" sound yes. (students all write g-l-a-d). http://www.youtube.com/watch?v=-K6bjT0Vxvc&feature=related

T = teacher; S = student; Ss= all students in unison.

The evaluation of students in example 1 is limited to compliance with this specific version of what it means to be a good reader: recognizing words quickly and accurately. In fact, students who do not respond in rhythm with the teacher or in unison with their peers are required to try again to get their answer "right." Though this approach may be appealing because it is orderly and systematic, it does not have an obvious relationship to reading as a "meaning-making," "message-getting" process (Clay, 1991).

Example 2 uses an analytic approach in which students are asked to write words they know with support from the teacher (revised "gladiator" to "glad" for the purpose of the lesson), using letter/sound patterns they have learned. Students are asked to use what they know about letter patterns to encode words they want to write in a way that others will understand.

The evaluation of students in example 2 is based on how well they *use* what they know about letter/sound patterns in order to read and write words, rather than how well they perform the routine in unison.

It is no surprise that some students flourish in each program, and indeed some students will flourish in any program, but the difference between these examples should not be underestimated. In one, reading and writing are performed skills, the performance of which is an end in itself. In the other, reading and writing are *used* to *do* something: send/receive a message, encode/decode words in order to communicate. It is possible to have all reading instruction, even skill practice, linked to reading for meaning, but this is not always the case.

The need for ensuring every reader—even those who cannot yet read independently—reads and writes for understanding on a daily basis seems almost too obvious to mention. And yet, some of the most popular core reading programs in the nation leave little room for actual reading; the nation's most powerful authorities on reading instruction question the value of independent reading time, and mounting evidence suggests that teachers' beliefs about their students' potential has an impact on whether they ever provide the opportunity for students to read texts they understand or develop comprehensive strategies.

This chapter describes two basic reasons why reading for understanding is so often ignored. They are followed by suggestions for ways to invest in daily reading for understanding.

REASON #1: THERE'S TOO MUCH OTHER STUFF TO DO

A study of six leading core reading programs found that teachers' editions outlined a elementary school reading block that allocated less than a quarter of the typical 90-minute period for students to read (Brenner & Hiebert, 2010). Time allocated for reading in third grade ranged from 10.2 minutes to 24.4 minutes with an average of 15 minutes of reading per day.

Even if students did have the opportunity to read more from their core program texts, there is little guarantee that such programs would provide texts students could understand and read themselves. In fact, there is evidence that students provided with only grade level, rather than independent level, texts do not have a rich diet of texts they understand and therefore make little progress.

For example, O'Connor et al. (2002) investigated the effect of two tutoring program models provided to struggling sixth grade students who read, on average, on a third grade level. One group of students was tutored using a sixth grade core text for English and/or social studies, while another group was tutored using third grade–level materials. Those who were tutored using grade level rather than independent-level texts—texts they could read with more than 95 percent accuracy—showed minimal progress, and those that were tutored using texts they could understand on their own made significant gains.

When teachers' guides present materials and schedules containing more than 75 percent reading-related "stuff" (activities other than reading for meaning), teachers have to ignore or replace them in order to provide the experiences students need to develop as readers. That is not to say that reading, language arts, or English classes do not have room for things like discussion, writing, representing text in images or actions, and so forth.

It is to say that there is very little room for low-level worksheets, cross-word puzzles, word searches, fill-in-the-blank sentences, and multiple-guess tests that come with so many textbooks or are printed off for so many trade books as a way to keep students busy and take up time.

The aspects of reading that are skill-driven (vocabulary, decoding, fluency) do require practice, but isolated practice is always less powerful than practice connected to reading for understanding.

What Is Driving Reading Instruction?

Core programs and curriculum guides that outline instructional priorities for teachers exist for four main reasons: (1) they provide resources that thoughtful teachers can use in flexible ways, (2) they provide guidelines for instruction that could raise the minimum proficiency of teachers who have yet to develop expertise in a certain curricular area, (3) they allow teachers across schools/districts/states to teach a uniform curriculum with similar methods, (4) they are enormously lucrative for publishing companies.

When it comes to the first reason, the time allocated for reading in a teacher's guide should not matter if individual teachers are permitted to apply their professional judgment and to reallocate time and resources to benefit their students.

Likewise, with the second and third reasons, if core programs and curriculum guides are used as a *guide*, rather than rigid requirements, they can be interpreted in ways that blend with and support professional judgment, respond to individual students, and still maintain a common core of educational experiences for students who transfer schools. This is what Valencia et al. (2001) described as curricula acting as "scaffolds" rather than as "shackles" for teachers.

When it comes to the relative weight of the fourth reason, it is important to keep the industrial machine of educational publishing at the forefront of your mind. Core reading programs often come full of activity and workbooks, assessment tools and isolated skill activities that require minimal reading and minimal writing simply because such resources are easy and cheap for publishers to produce and monitor.

It is hard to package instruction that guides students to read and write interesting and appropriate texts for authentic purposes. It is even more difficult to measure that sort of instruction, which is why there are far more commercially available tests of decoding, word recognition and fluency than there are of comprehension.

Educational publishing and educational testing are both multimillion dollar industries, and they depend on each other, as do the related markets of test preparation, consulting, and data management. In fact each of these markets can be made to feed each other so that schools are in a constant cycle of needing to buy more of something (assessments, materials, consulting) in order not to look like they are "failing."

As Kelly Gallagher (2009) wrote, WYTIWYG: What you test is what you get. If teachers are held accountable for students' progress on tests of isolated skills and the reading of decontextualized passages with no purpose for reading—or worse, a timed list of nonsense words—that is what they will spend time preparing students to do. Such activities supplant real reading because teachers feel pressured to prioritize them given the tests that have been purchased from publishers.

Commercial programs that provide contrived, isolated skills practice and low-level worksheets can be viewed as creating the reading difficulties their other products purport to solve. People with the non-negotiables, not marketing pitches, in mind should ruthlessly review commercial products before purchase.

As Elaine Garan (2002) has pointed out, there are close personal (and business) relationships between many of the individuals who create commercial test prep materials and curricular materials, and those who mandate the use of certain curricula or testing through legislation.

For example, the presidential Bush family is close friends and neighbors with the McGraw family of McGraw-Hill Publishing, which happens to sell reading curricula and assessments. George W. Bush's administration is responsible for No Child Left Behind's (NCLB) focus on adopting certain reading curricula and mandating annual testing. McGraw-Hill, among many others, markets such materials.

McGraw-Hill is a "leading global financial information and education company" with more than $6 billion in annual sales (McGraw-Hill.com). So, even though the name is closely associated with educational publishing, they also have other interests to preserve: for example, their financial information division, which goes under the name "Standard & Poors," as in "the S&P 500."

When it comes to describing the role of "big business" interests in education, "big" seems too small a word. Pointing this out is by no means an indictment on the company or its materials, but a simple reminder that large and powerful forces are at work when programs are designed, bought, sold, mandated, and evaluated. *Someone* always benefits when curricular materials are sold, but it is necessary to ask whether it is ever the children these materials are meant to serve.

What About Test Prep?

Test preparation has a place, but, contrary to popular myth, that place is both known and specific: up to 30 percent of class time, no more than ten weeks before the test. John Guthrie's research on methods of test preparation found that five components had varying impact on a student's test performance: reading ability, content knowledge, motivation, test format, and error (Guthrie, 2002). By comparing student performance across a range of tests and test items, Guthrie was able to attribute relative impact to each of these components (see figure 2).

Not surprisingly, reading ability is a better predictor than any other component. Many might be surprised to know that motivation contributes almost as much as error to a student's score and that knowledge of format contributes much less. Guthrie argues that classroom instruction should be divided among the contributing components in equal proportion to their importance. That is, the largest part should be actual reading instruction, the next largest should be devoted to content knowledge development, the next largest to motivation and so on.

Given their relative importance, 20 percent of time within ten weeks of a high stakes assessment should be spent on general strategies for test-taking

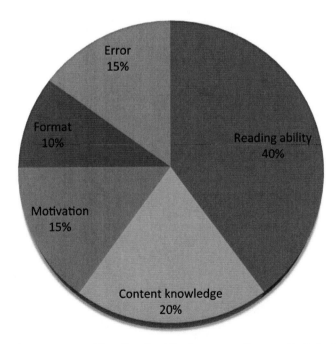

Figure 2. Components of Reading Test Performance. Source: Guthrie, 2002. Used with permission.

and question interpretation. Ten percent of the time during the ten-week period before the test should be spent familiarizing students with the test's format. Any more than this may desensitize students to the actual test format (they may over-expect certain formats and struggle when they change). The majority of the time leading up to the test, and all of the rest of the year should be spent on motivating reading and content instruction.

When this is not the case—when test preparation activities take up an hour a week all year, or part of every period, or all day every day leading up to a test—opportunities to develop literacy are supplanted by activities that have never been shown to improve reading ability. Students' scores reflect this and schools too often respond by insisting on more test prep, more tests, and more data analysis rather than more coherent, meaning-driven, motivating instruction.

Reading Instruction and the National Reading Panel

Another reason for limited investment in reading for meaning on a daily basis may be the mixed research on independent reading programs highlighted in the recommendations of the federally-appointed National Reading Panel (NRP). The NRP reported that:

> Even though encouraging students to read more is intuitively appealing, there is still not sufficient research evidence obtained from studies of high methodological quality to support the idea that such efforts reliably increase how much students read or that such programs result in improved reading skills. (n.p.)

The NRPs findings were used to create and market an entire generation of curricular materials and intervention programs as well as in the design of teacher preparation and professional development. The aspects of reading they *did* find support for are often referred to as, "the five pillars" of reading instruction. These are the star players in all manner of commercially available programs and products for learning to read.

The five pillars include phonological awareness, phonics, fluency, vocabulary, and comprehension, in that order and, to the exclusion of other possible "pillars." For instance, as will be discussed in chapter 5, writing was left out of their report due to time constraints rather than relative importance. Several prominent reading researchers have suggested that if those five are "pillars" of effective instruction, there are at least five (Allington, 2005) or 20 (Shanahan, 2003) others that are just important, but were not included.

For better and for worse, those five pillars were set out to guide and measure all reading instruction. Since they were given equal weight and equal billing in the report, they are often given equal weight and equal time in curricular materials. That means that comprehension, rather than being positioned as the goal that should underlie all reading instruction (including skill-building), is merely one of five equally important things—three of which, Paris (2005) argued, develop early in reading acquisition and are thus less and less important for instruction as readers develop.

For example, if students can decode accurately, we can assume phonological awareness is intact and no longer needs explicit instruction or instructional time. Likewise decoding and fluency are more finite than vocabulary (limitless) and comprehension (endless) with a "ceiling" on trajectories of development.

At a certain point, it is not desirable to read any faster or with greater expression and not possible to read with any more accuracy. On the other hand, it is always possible to learn more about words and how they work (vocabulary becomes word analysis, semantics, and semiotics) and to think more critically about meaning (comprehension becomes analysis and criticism).

Vocabulary and comprehension are perhaps the most powerful and important of the five pillars, but they come last in the report and have equal billing with the first three. In fact, they have less than equal billing in the widely distributed NRP summary report (National Educators Association, 2012). This has opened the doors to programs that address each individual pillar rather than insisting on their integration for the purpose of comprehension. For specific examples of what instruction wrapped in meaning might look like see table 3.2 or tables 8.1 and 8.2 in the final chapter.

There has been some resistance and negative reaction to the summary of the NRP report (for discussions of this see Garan, 2002; Garan, 2004, Allington, 2002), but its influence is still pervasive. After 2001, programs that did not bear the "research-based" sticker on them practically would not sell. The No Child Left Behind Act (NCLB, 2001) required federally funded programs to focus on the "five essential components of reading" as outlined by the NRP (PL 107-110, Title I, Part B, Subpart 1) and mandated the exclusive use of "scientifically based reading research" as defined by the panel.

The phrase "scientifically based research" appears in the text of NCLB no fewer than 111 times. It was nice for the government to claim that their program only "focuses on proven methods of early reading instruction," but it spent literally no time investigating such methods for middle or high school reading instruction or instruction for special populations. Still, the NRP report was the arbiter of what counted as "scientifically based research" even when teachers and researchers found themselves divided.

For example, there has long been a debate about the relative value of activities designed to increase time spent reading for meaning like Sustained Silent Reading (SSR) or Drop Everything And Read (DEAR) or Independent Reading (IR). Research on the value of long periods of independent reading is mixed, not because time spent reading is not effective, but because allotting time to reading does not guarantee the intensity of practice.

Table 3.2. Instruction Wrapped in Meaning Making

Component of reading	Isolated instruction	Instruction wrapped in meaning making
Decoding	Wrote memorization of letter-sound patterns, word spellings, stacks of flash cards for word recognition without linking these patterns to words and phrases that carry meaning.	Students use what they know about letter patterns to write meaningful messages to specific people/things. Students learn new spelling patterns in the context of words they know and use.
Fluency	Repeated reading of a contrived passage. Choral reading of a passage with no discussion of its meaning or importance.	Repeated readings of things that are important because they are so important (quotes, speeches, punchlines). Opportunities to perform plays, poems or prose, with time to rehearse and discuss pace and prosody for clear communication.
Vocabulary	Copying dictionary definitions, filling in blanks, completing word searches.	Learning words in context by learning their relationships with other words, concepts, settings. Repeated exposure to target words includes finding them in context, using them in writing or speech, comparing what a word is used to mean in different settings.
Comprehension	Assign-assess cycle of postreading, low-level multiple choice questions.	A cycle of reading and discussion, the opportunity to act out or draw what you've read, or to take some action in response to it.
Motivation	Students engage with text out of fear of disciplinary action, or to earn unrelated, extrinsic prizes (more recess, candy, money).	Students engage with texts they find meaningful or that can be used to do something meaningful (reading a manual to build a toy, reading a second book by a favorite author to see if it's as good as the first, reading to learn more about something you like to do, preparing to talk to a peer about what you're reading).

Given 20 minutes of SSR some students may read 19 minutes and 59 seconds worth of a text they can and want to read (good practice!) while others read less than one minute. Sometimes avoidance takes the shape of long stints of "choosing what to read." Sometimes it takes the shape of misbehavior, sleeping, long water breaks, or even absences. Often, it takes

the shape of holding a book but looking at or thinking about any and everything else.

Unfortunately, it is most likely that the readers who use the time most
efficiently and get the most effective practice are the students who are already good readers. That does not mean that giving readers time to read is not
important. It is "necessary but not sufficient," mostly due to differences
between *allocated* and *actual* time, as well as optimal or inappropriate text
difficulty.

If this is the case, the NRP is right; there is little evidence that allocating
time for independent reading is the cause of reading growth. And there's
little reason to believe that it should be, if independent reading time can mean
everything from sleeping with a book in hand to reading something engross-
ing, interesting, and meaningful.

In the end, the question the NRP answered with their review of empirical
research was not the important one to ask. Rather than asking, "Does reading
volume increase reading achievement," they asked, "Do independent reading
programs reliably increase reading achievement." The answer was no, and
the result was less support for teachers or programs willing to invest time in
independent reading. It is not, after all, one of the five pillars—it is not even
"research based."

Just like trees need sunlight and water, promising instructional approaches need more than just allocated time to be effective. For example,
independent reading needs students to have texts they can and want to read,
as well as an environment that supports their desire to do so. Among other
things, promising instructional approaches also require teachers who believe
they can help their students learn. This brings us to the next possible reason
that reading for understanding is so often replaced by other activities.

REASON #2: ADULTS DO NOT BELIEVE STUDENTS CAN READ FOR MEANING

A large body of research suggests that teachers' beliefs about struggling
readers have an impact on their expectations for student success (e.g.,
McGill-Franzen, 1994), the instruction they provide (Scharlach, 2008; Mallette, Readence, McKinney & Smith, 2000) and their sense of responsibility
for teaching struggling readers (Winfield, 1986).

In her in-depth case studies of pre-service teachers engaged in a one-to-
one reading tutoring program, Tabitha Scarlach (2008) found that there were
two recognizable patterns among those enrolled in a reading specialist certification program. Some pre-service teachers did not believe it was their job to
teach all children to read, felt ill-prepared to do so (low teacher self-effica-

cy), and positioned themselves as "suppliers" rather than "coaches" during tutoring sessions.

Despite training and ongoing coaching, this group consistently failed to select appropriate materials or provide adequate "wait time" after a student miscued or paused while reading. They were quick to correct the student, but less likely to give them time to try or teach a strategy that would help them do it on their own.

They attributed their students' existing difficulties to lack of motivation or behavior issues. If students failed to make progress during the tutoring program, they attributed this to a reading disability. The pre-service teachers in this category often reported that it was the job of a parent or resource teacher (not a classroom teacher) to teach students with reading disabilities. Rather than try their best anyway, they failed to provide the kind of instruction they were taught to give.

Other teachers in Scarlach's study reported believing that it was their responsibility to teach struggling readers, and also reported believing they could do it (higher teacher self-efficacy). Scarlach's analysis of their tutoring sessions and related documents demonstrated that these pre-service teachers took responsibility for student success and failures, attributing both to their instruction, and, they consistently modified their instructional approaches accordingly. These teachers were more likely to choose appropriate texts, wait for a student to self-correct, and to model or prompt the use of strategies (coach) while students read.

Thus, teachers who believed their students could learn to read, and that they could help, acted in ways that made this a self-fulfilling prophecy. Those that did not share this belief in students or themselves acted in ways that created failure, often by limiting opportunities for students to read appropriate texts with strategies for comprehension.

Unfortunately, teachers can easily find support for the belief that young or struggling readers cannot read for meaning from reductionist approaches to remediation and vestiges of "reading readiness" perspectives on reading development.

From this perspective, instruction cannot proceed until students have demonstrated mastery of a set of prerequisite skills that showed they were "ready." That is, once students have demonstrated mastery of foundational skills, more complex or integrated skills (like comprehension) should be taught. Unfortunately for some students, this might be years down the road, in which case their reading instruction might consist of skill building with no meaning making for years at a time.

In the 1980s there was a paradigm shift away from readiness philosophies, guided by Marie Clay's writing on emergent literacy (Teale & Sulzby, 1986). Like example 2 from the contrasting classroom exchanges at the beginning of this chapter, an emergent literacy perspective has a focus on increasing control over the functions of print. On the other hand, a readiness perspective focuses on the form of print: with handwriting and letter formation taken as indications of readiness to read, and reading taken as evidence of readiness to write.

As Erickson (2000) pointed out, the emergent literacy perspective was vital to the education of students who, for a range of reasons, struggled to display conventional indicators of literacy learning. She argued that acknowledging the possibility of unconventional indicators of competence provides a way to recognize and build upon the strengths of students with disability labels.

For example, some students may struggle with letter formation because of a physical challenge, but understand sound-symbol correspondences and spelling patterns well enough to read or select letters for writing. Some other students may not accurately produce speech sounds associated with print, but understand them well. Assessment and instruction from an emergent perspective notes and honors the strengths students bring to literacy even when their strengths do not fit a checklist of ordered indicators.

Despite the paradigm shift towards emergent literacy perspectives in K–12 education, there are still vestiges of the readiness in the form of rigid sequences of expected development, and the idea that readers *get to* comprehension by mastering the associated skills. On the contrary, we now have very strong evidence that even preschool-aged students can benefit from explicit comprehension instruction in the context of read alouds and shared reading (Cunningham & Shaugory, 2005).

Even before they can identify letters, children can comprehend stories and can demonstrate their understanding of text structure and connections between texts by acting them out, drawing, and talking about them.

Meaning, decoding and fluency exist in a *reciprocal, not causal* relationship with each supporting the other. Knowing what the sentence means (comprehension) helps readers make better guesses and predictions about each word (decoding) and helps them decide the appropriate rhythm and inflection for it (fluency).

Assuming Competence

Even readers who do not yet demonstrate conventional literacy are capable of making meaning from text, especially when we take a broad definition of text. Reading, at its core, is making meaning from symbols. Symbols and symbolic relationships exist around us in the world in many more places than the printed page.

If students have yet to master decoding, they can make meaning by discussing stories that are read to them, or creating stories from picture books without words. They can write using whatever combination of words, images and symbols are currently within their repertoire. Leaving time for students to interpret images or draw-write stories is not settling for something that is less than real reading or writing; it is acknowledging current efforts towards reading and writing. Only when they are acknowledged can they be extended.

Older learners may be reluctant to engage in activities that use their developing skills to make or express meaning because it may seem childish or unsophisticated. In these cases it is important to draw upon all the many ways in which we "read" the world around us.

We "read" signs, warnings, facial expressions, cloud formations, comics, graphic novels, and other patterned symbols in ways that involve, but do not depend on, conventional reading and writing. Many of these ways of reading the world are already well developed among older readers, and can be used as touchstones and metaphors for the development of similar skills with print.

Lastly, investing time and attention on students' unconventional and/or nonprint uses of literacy and literate thought demonstrates your presumption of a student's competence—a "gift" that is too often withheld from diverse learners, with great consequence to their sense of self-efficacy, worth, and intelligence.

If we position readers as already literate, and working on extending their existing abilities to conventional use of a print-based system, they approach literacy learning as competent beings, rather than disabled learners, and will progress accordingly. If instead we position readers as deficient and disabled, they may have few opportunities to approach learning experiences any other way, and will progress accordingly.

We not only have to believe that everyone *can* learn to read, we have to begin to take multiple pathways to and expressions of literacy seriously to maintain a focus on reading as meaning-making.

This means being aware that there are many unsanctioned ways people have successfully learned to read, and it means allowing students who struggle with traditional pathways to show us new or alternate pathways. We do this by allowing students to demonstrate their competence even if this competence is not listed on an official checklist of skills. This means noticing their interests, successes, and ways of learning so that we can imagine ways to make conventional literacy an extension of their existing competence.

WHAT YOU SHOULD SEE IN A CLASSROOM WITH A FOCUS ON MEANING

1. Literacy activities always have a stated purpose. No one learns to read so that they can recite word recognition tasks or read along with a

stopwatch. Both teachers and students should be able to tell or show you why they are reading/writing what they are reading/writing.

2. Students are found reading independently on a regular basis (daily or weekly). When they do, they should be able to answer the following:

    a. *Why are you reading this?*

- Note that having a purpose* (especially a meaningful purpose) suggests a greater possibility that students will be engaged and develop their belief that reading can be meaningful.

    b. *What are you reading about?*
    c. *What can you do with this text? Or what/who is it written for?*
    d. *What do you plan to read next?*

3. Students are assessed based on how well they *use* literacy skills, rather than how well they "perform" them.

    a. Ability is judged by how well students use literacy-related skills to accomplish things that are important to them, rather than working towards the contrived performance of isolated skills or contrived academic tasks.

4. Teachers describe what students *can* do, rather than what they cannot yet do.

    a. If this seems like a spurious attempt at political correctness, consider that instruction can only ever begin at square one when we assume students "can't" do something. If we are specific about what they can do, or try to do, we have a much more accurate and specific starting point for instruction, as well as clues about how students might make progress.

5. Whether or not time and access to text exist out of school, students report being willing to use their own time to read because they see its inherent value.

*A note on "purpose for reading": State standards on "author's purpose" have often limited conversations about purposes for reading to posters that say, "PIE" (persuade, inform, entertain). That is because standardized tests designed to assess these well-meaning standards routinely require students to select whether a passage was likely written to persuade, inform or entertain them.

Instruction aligns with assessment, and test preparation reproduces assessment, so students can grow up thinking there are three reasons to read/ three reasons authors wrote, neither of which are particularly tied to anything that gives goosebumps or changes one's worldview. Purposes for reading are taught by examples and experiences of purposeful reading, not by picking one of three options.

WAYS TO INVEST IN DAILY READING FOR UNDERSTANDING

1. Design skills instruction within meaningful contexts (see table 3.1)
2. Generate examples of people across cultures and fields that have used literacies in important ways outside of school. Allow students to add to this list of examples and to try out the formats and genres they see in use among adults they admire.
3. Assign or accept writing in a range of formats and genres, and draw attention to the communicative impact of decisions about the formats and features students incorporate into their own writing.

   a. For example, in addition to structured paragraphs and five-paragraph essays, include: post cards, invoices, encyclopedia entries, reviews, news articles, memos, invitations, sets of directions, comics, captioned illustrations, etc.

POINTS FOR DISCUSSION

Ask yourself and others:

1. What do the materials and instructional routines in use in our setting imply is the purpose of reading?
2. What do the assessments in use in our setting demonstrate to students about what it means to read well?
3. What are the reasons for reading and writing that students encounter in my course?
4. What reasons for reading and writing go along with the "real world" or professional version of my discipline (science, social studies, math, etc.)?

Chapter Four

Every Reading Intervention Is Balanced to Incorporate Meaning

Even when classroom instruction includes time for comprehension and reading for meaning, interventions designed to remediate reading difficulty are sometimes stripped of meaning and context so that they can target a specific area of difficulty. For example, students might practice reading nonsense words to apply decoding skills, answer batteries of multiple-choice questions for comprehension, practice reading the same uninteresting text over and over again for fluency, or segment and blend words for twenty minutes without linking those words to meaning or communicative expression.

The problem with isolating skills from meaningful contexts is that engagement and motivation to read, as well as the transfer of these skills to real reading, may be compromised. When students demonstrate the need for targeted instruction or extra practice with an individual skill, a *balanced approach*, one in which skills practice always comes with opportunities to read for meaning, is non-negotiable.

WHY A "BALANCED APPROACH" TO INTERVENTION DESIGN IS NON-NEGOTIABLE

How do we know a balanced approach to intervention design is non-negotiable? We can actually see it. In order to see what brains look like while reading, researchers use neuroimaging tools like functional-MRI technology, which requires people to lie very still in a tunnel while they perform tasks (like word recognition) in response to words or directions on a screen.

fMRIs measure brain activity by detecting changes in blood flow within different regions of the brain. They can map these measurements onto images of the brain using color-coding to show the degree of activation. This shows researchers which parts have the most or least flow. Similarly, EEG (electro-encephalography) technology has been used to measure brain activity by recording electrical activity via a large number of sensors placed along some-one's scalp. This doesn't require entering a spaceship-like tunnel, but does involve a hairnet full of sensors.

Though neursoscientists consider this line of neuroimaging research on reading difficulty to be in its infancy relative to other areas of inquiry (Pugh, 2011), it already has some important implications for practice. For example, in 2009 Keller and Just used a form of MRI technology (diffusion tensor imaging) to measure the organization of white matter in the brains of chil-dren who struggled with reading. After 100 hours of intervention sessions, the microstructural organization of that region increased in ways that sug-gested neural pathways had been myelinated (insulated) and were therefore more organized and efficient.

These interventions involved a combination of programs designed to pro-vide intensive, systematic instruction in all five pillars of reading. That com-bination of instruction made a visible difference in the cortical structures of students' brains.

Similarly, in 2003 Alyward and colleagues used fMRI technology to map activation patterns in typical readers and dyslexic readers before and after the dyslexic readers participated in an intervention. This intervention consisted of only twenty-eight hours of instruction, but scientists still observed a change in the activation patterns in the brains of students with dyslexia labels.

The intervention in this case was designed to be "comprehensive" in its approach to the NRP's "five pillars," not solely focused isolated skills. In this case, students' posttest pattern of activation looked exactly like the pattern of their typically developing peers.

In another study, Shaywitz and colleagues (2003) showed that some stu-dents who struggle to learn to read throughout their school years developed compensatory activation patterns that were different from typically develop-ing peers. Shaywitz argues that compensatory patterns are not as efficient as typically developing strategies, but still allow students with persistent diffi-culty to eventually learn to read (often with less fluency).

Taken together, these studies suggest that even when there is a neurologi-cal basis for reading difficulty, the brain can (re)organize for reading—one way or another—when provided with interventions that are balanced to in-clude comprehension instruction and reading for meaning along with instruc-tion on component skills.

WHAT WE DO AND DO NOT KNOW FROM NEUROIMAGING

There is more to reading than what we can see using neuroimaging technology. In fact the danger of relying on neuroimaging alone to validate intervention programs, besides the time it will take, is that we might succumb to the unfortunate view that reading is a mechanical and mostly biological process. This view is unfortunate because it has a couple of inherent dangers.

First, we may assume that reading difficulty is "hard wired" in the sense that it is inevitable and cannot be changed. On the contrary, neuroscientists often point out that reading acquisition, unlike language acquisition, is *not* a natural process that anyone is automatically predisposed to learn. Moreover, the plasticity of the brain—its ability to change and adapt—has consistently been demonstrated in neuroimaging studies of reading interventions (e.g., Gabrieli, 2009; Shaywitz & Shaywitz, 2007).

Second, we may assume that reading difficulty with a neurological substrate always requires intervention from medical doctors or other specialized experts (not parents or teachers). Many neuroimaging studies of reading interventions that have demonstrated positive changes included familiar interventions conducted by teachers or reading specialists (e.g., Keller & Just, 2009).

Finally, reading (like communication) is often identified as biological because we do it with our bodies (eyes, brain). And yet, the social, affective and emotional aspects of reading (engagement, confidence, motivation) shouldn't be underestimated—even and especially for those who struggle with reading.

Here is what *is* clear from the neuroscience literature:

1. Every brain can (re)organize for reading.
2. Balanced interventions work.

    a. Unbalanced interventions may not work (more on this later).

3. A focus on meaning matters even for those who struggle with the fundamentals (decoding, spelling, word recognition).

WHAT WE KNOW ABOUT INTERVENTIONS THAT WORK

Balanced Means Basic Skills Are Not Separate from Meaning Making

Perhaps the most important takeaway from brain imaging studies is that instruction that balances the five pillars has made measureable differences in brain structure and activation. Indeed a review of existing intervention programs will show that those whose explicit skill instruction is wrapped in meaning making are predictably more engaging and more effective than those with a narrower focus. There is even some evidence that attending only to fluency or decoding tasks can have a negative impact on comprehension.

For example twelve of the twenty-four reading intervention programs reviewed by the What Works Clearinghouse had "no discernable effects" or a "negative" impact on overall reading achievement, even though each of these studies had a positive impact on at least one subskill of reading (print awareness, phonemic awareness, alphabetics).

This might be because teaching any one subskill for its own sake may register changes in that subskill, but will not transfer to overall reading achievement unless the intervention itself engages all aspects of reading. It also might be because time spent on narrow intervention activities supplanted exposure to text and/or negated motivation to read. Even when intervening at the earliest stages of literacy development, a balance between the five pillars (with all aspects of instruction wrapped in meaning making and grounded in a motivational purpose) are more effective than narrowly focusing on one pillar or another.

In addition, large-scale studies of teachers who "beat the odds" and consistently led struggling readers to make significant gains in reading achievement, despite variables like class size and poverty, have consistently highlighted a focus on meaning as the defining feature of exemplary teaching (Knapp et al., 1995; Langer, 2001; Taylor & Pearson, 2002). Though few would argue against infusing meaning into interventions, this is often the first thing to go when intervention programs are packaged, delivered by a computer or overseen by someone who lacks expertise in reading.

Teacher Expertise

Researchers have found that struggling readers often receive the least and least expert instruction of all students. In many cases, children who are pulled out for reading help miss out on important classroom instruction, and spend substantial amounts of their intervention time transitioning from the classroom to a different teacher and setting, only to have to pack up early to transition back (McGill-Franzen & Allington, 1990).

Researchers have also found that students in lower reading groups were more likely to be assigned to work with an instructional aide (IA) than a certified teacher, and are more likely to be interrupted or corrected while they read (Allington, 1981, 2009).

Additionally, class size reduction studies that compare the impact of teachers compared to instructional assistants (who generally have less training and presumably less expertise in reading pedagogy) demonstrate that teacher expertise makes a large difference in student achievement (Nye,

Konstapoulus, & Hedges, 2004). Though no one can guarantee that a certain degree or certification equates with actual expertise or effectiveness, there is evidence that knowing more about reading makes a difference for student outcomes.

For example, in McGill-Franzen and colleagues' 1999 study of kindergarten literacy instruction, all teachers received new classroom libraries, but only half of the teachers received training on using the new materials. The teachers with additional training had significantly better outcomes, especially among at-risk readers.

In a later study (described in McGill-Franzen, 2007), the addition of professional development in reading for kindergarten teachers increased outcomes for students who received interventions as well as the overall achievement of the entire class, and these positive differences in achievement were still evident when the students were tested in the third grade.

Similarly, Scanlon and Sweeney (2010) found that providing kindergarten teachers with professional development in reading instruction improved the average reading achievement of all their students, and especially the most struggling readers.

Professional development isn't all high-quality, and teacher preparation programs do not always have a discernible impact on teachers' performance. Still, there is undeniable evidence that knowing more about children and reading makes teachers more likely to help more children learn to read. Investing in the development of teacher expertise is never a bad investment, especially when the professional development is designed to succeed (see appendix B for high-quality professional development selection criteria).

Teacher Beliefs

Assuming competence and closely observing and extending individual students' attempts at literacy are at the very core of *expert* remedial instruction. Yet, not all students are presumed to be capable of learning to read. Phillips, Hayward, and Norris (2011) have argued that the fact of a disability label (e.g., dyslexia) sometimes causes teachers to underestimate a student's potential, which is the first step in creating or sustaining difficulty where it need not exist. Spear-Swerling and Sternberg (1996) have also demonstrated that students with disability labels often struggle due to lack of appropriate instruction, rather than any personal problem with reading.

Too often, when difficulty is assumed to lie within students' *brains*, it is pathologized and then sidestepped or avoided. Allington (2011), personal communication) describes this phenomenon as "teacher-created disability" because difficulty is exacerbated or created by a lack of appropriate instruction. Given the range of adults who may be involved in providing literacy instruction during a school day (Croninger & Valli, 2009) it may be more appropriate to use the term "school-created" disabilities. Either way, the fact remains that plenty of students struggle because of factors within educators' control.

In the mid-1990s Spear-Swerling and Sternberg warned that providing a label for difficulty is not always the same thing as addressing the difficulty. They wrote,

> learning-disabilities terminology relieved schools and parents of any respon-
> sibility for children's learning problems, without stigmatizing children as egre-
> giously as older special-education terminology had done. It was as though
> naming a pattern of behavior somehow explained that pattern. (p. 38)

They argued further that students with disability labels may be more likely to be met with instruction that matches the disability label, rather than the individual, and that this too often leads to continued difficulty. As Phillips and Smith (2010) have written, "If the hardest-to-teach children (have) not yet learned how to read and write, it (is) because we, the educators, (have) not yet learned how to teach them" (p. 221).

We have strong evidence that upwards of 95 percent of children can learn to read in elementary school if early signs of difficulty are met with expert reading interventions. This is the evidence that inspired response to intervention (RTI) models. But, as materials for RTI approaches are developed, commercialized and sold in the educational publishing market, interventions may more often be packaged and standardized rather than individualized and delivered with expertise.

The same principle is true with special education placements as an intervention for reading difficulty. As McKinney (1989) has demonstrated, the fact of providing special education instruction (or any given intervention) is not enough to guarantee a dramatic increase in access to appropriate instruction or opportunity to learn. In his three-year longitudinal study, special education placements for children with learning disability labels did not close gaps in rate of growth or achievement in reading relative to regular education peers.

When compared with reviews of research on reading interventions outside of special education classes (e.g., Torgesen, 2000), McKinney's results suggest that the special education placements in his study did not provide more, more personalized or more expert reading instruction and therefore did not dramatically change students' rate or trajectory of achievement.

Studies that *have* demonstrated close to 100 percent success in ensuring every child is a reader did not rely on packaged programs; they used intensive one-to-one tutoring provided by expert instructors. Even when interventions included ideas and materials from commercially available programs, expert tutors were expected to be responsive to the student, not the prescribed curriculum.

For example, in 2000, Torgesen reviewed five studies of reading interventions and estimated that current methods would leave only 2–5 percent of students without adequate word reading skills by the end of second grade. In each case, teachers worked with struggling readers for at least twenty minutes, four times a week in a one-to-one setting. In summary, Torgesen wrote "a large proportion (always more than 50 percent) of children who are most at risk for reading failure can be helped to learn at roughly normal rates in early elementary school by applying the best of what we know right now about reading instruction" (p. 51).

Later, Torgesen (2006) explained that in a longitudinal study (also see Torgesen et al., 2001), a special education class seemed only sufficient to maintain students' levels of reading deficiency (they neither improved nor decreased their rate of reading acquisition in the special education setting). Yet an intensive one-to-one intervention was sufficient to dramatically increase students' rates of reading acquisition. Within a year of the eight-week intervention, 40 percent of students were declassified and had returned to regular education classes.

Given that most public school calendars include about thirty-six weeks of instruction, we might consider assigning expert interventionists to work intensely with individual students over short periods of time, rather than distributing their attention (and minimizing their impact) across a group of students all year.

It may be that the same staff could support a larger number of students with much more efficient and robust results if they scheduled shorter periods of time (eight to twelve weeks) with individual students. Fortunately, the reauthorized version of IDEA (2004) explicitly directed schools to use up to 15 percent of the special education budget for the prevention of reading difficulties. Hiring a handful of expert reading teachers, and/or investing in existing teachers' reading expertise, would be a smarter investment of such funds than buying into packaged commercial programs that merely simulate tiered support.

In fact, Scanlon and Sweeney (2010) found that providing classroom teachers with professional development that deepened reading expertise was more effective than providing expert interventions only to the students that struggled with reading. Providing both professional development and expert tutoring was the most powerful condition, but the impact of investing in the classroom teacher's expertise had the largest individual impact on students' trajectories of achievement. (See appendix B for guidance on selecting high-quality professional development.)

WHAT YOU SHOULD SEE WHEN OBSERVING A READING INTERVENTION PROGRAM

1. Students read texts as part of the program.

   a. Even if they have not yet mastered decoding, students can make meaning out of short, simple, repetitive sentences using picture cues or reading after someone models the passage. They may also read back their own writing.

      • Though this may look like copying or memorizing, it solidifies the habit of matching voice to print and may solidify strategies for word recognition and the use of meaning- or illustration-based (visual) cueing systems.

   b. Though direct instruction on isolated skills may take up part of instructional time, this is not disconnected from real reading of texts that are interesting (humorous, meaningful, relevant).

2. The match between reader and text allows for high-success reading experiences.

   a. This may involve repeated readings of a familiar text or text on various levels

3. Students talk, draw, or write about what they read to ensure they are reading for meaning rather than only accuracy.
4. Students are aware of the progress they are making and their goals for intervention time.

   a. This supports a sense of agency and directs students' focus during sessions.
   b. Visibly tracking progress builds self-efficacy and motivation to continue.

5. Students can move at their own pace, but still make progress.

   a. The whole point of an intervention is individualized, targeted instruction. If funding and scheduling require interventions to be delivered in small groups, rather than one to one, students should still be able to move at their own pace, skipping aspects of the program that don't apply to their particular set of strengths and challenges.

   b. Texts and activities should not be so difficult that students can't finish them on their own or stay on the same task until frustrated.

POINTS FOR DISCUSSION (WHEN REVIEWING A POTENTIAL INTERVENTION PROGRAM)

1. If there is evidence that this program has worked before, where does the evidence come from, and what sorts of populations and contexts is it based on?

   a. Most of the studies that qualified for the NRP review were based on relatively small samples of low-achieving students and students with reading disability labels between first and sixth grade (Garan, 2002). No English language learners, children in grade 7 or above, and very few typically developing or gifted readers were included. That doesn't mean we should discount the research, but it does mean we can't raise a finger in the air and pronounce, "Research says . . ." with such certainty. Research may *suggest* this is useful for certain populations, but it cannot guarantee usefulness with yours. Understanding the studies that led people to support a given approach may help you decide if it is a good fit for your students or not.

2. If the program includes reading texts (and it should) what are the texts? Where do they come from? Are they varied and interesting?

   a. This is the place where many programs fall short as it can be prohibitively expensive to buy copyrights to existing literature or pay talented writers to construct interesting leveled passages for the program. Not every selection has to be a masterpiece, but consider the impact of a steady diet of this type of text on your students' comprehension and motivation before you buy.

3. Is there a flexible but present scope and sequence that can be a support to teachers, but easily modified to fit students?

   a. Valencia et al. (2006) described reading curricula as either "shackles" or "scaffolds" for teachers learning to teach reading. Those that were allowed to draw upon curricular materials flexibly could use them as support for their planning and still deliver responsive instruction. Those who had no curricular materials or a strictly scripted program learned less about reading pedagogy and were less successful with their students after three years.

4. Does the intervention involve preassessment, formative assessment (may be informal), and postassessment?

   a. Interventions should be focused on the skill areas students need support in, not on activities that support areas of relative strength (see table 2.2).
   b. Instructors should be aware of students' relative strengths and should build on or relate to these areas of strength.
   c. Students should be aware of what they are working on and how they are making progress

5. Do the program's activities and routines allow a teacher/tutor to observe the student's thought process (e.g., listen to a student read aloud, ask them to tell you what they know about a text how they know it) and to model, coach, or intervene?

   a. Activities and routines should be designed to make students' knowledge and thought process available to the teacher to observe. Activities should require students to follow or display their approach to recognizing words, reading them fast and smooth, and making them make sense.

      • Programs that involve students reading to themselves and then answering questions may not provide a teacher with enough insight into the student's process to diagnose difficulty or confusion. Note: this knocks out most computer-based intervention programs.

For more information about selecting or evaluating reading intervention programs, please see appendix D: Answers to Frequently Asked Questions about Reading Interventions.

Chapter Five

Every Reader Writes about Something Meaningful

Graham and Hebert's 2010 meta-analysis of research on writing instruction concluded that there is robust and decisive evidence that reading and writing are reciprocal processes, and that time spent on writing instruction is important both for its role in writing development and for its contribution to literacy (reading, writing, communication) in general.

WHY WRITING IS NON-NEGOTIABLE:
READING, WRITING, RECIPROCITY

All aspects of reading are supportive of and supported by aspects of writing. For example, spelling is the inverse of decoding, and thus solidifies decoding skills and strategies by applying them in a different modality. Fluency is reflected in choices about punctuation and sentence structure and is thus implicitly built by composing text, and explicitly developed by increasing exposure to the written word.

Vocabulary is likewise solidified and even sometimes extended as students use words to *do* things, and thus find themselves using (not just memorizing) vocabulary, and searching for what the French call *le mot juste*: the perfect word. This not only increases their vocabulary size and word awareness, it helps students tune in to the word choices of authors they read, and thus make inferences about tone, mood, purpose and other elements of literary and rhetorical analysis.

Comprehension is perhaps the largest beneficiary of writing instruction as students learn to "read like writers" (Calkins, 1992) by noticing the subtle choices other authors make, and responding to them as readers. Writing

practice and instruction work to increase students' competence in every reading skill and therefore also increases motivation and engagement. Moreover,
it provides a different pathway to literacy that relies less on sound (and
therefore auditory processing) or receptive language competence. As the
expressive inverse of reading, writing is sometimes the reason students find
their way into literacy.

Finally, the writing process requires rereading— which is excellent reading practice. It is an ongoing struggle for older beginning readers to find
interesting, compelling, comprehensible input—that is, texts that can be
understood and are still worth reading. Yet, when students write and reread
their own writing, the text is automatically comprehensible, even if not conventional.

By revising and editing their own work, students incidentally read and
reread their self-created texts (thus solidifying what they know about those
words and building fluency) as they consider how others will make meaning
from it.

This is an especially important entry point for readers who have language
delays, are learning English, have limited access to speech sounds (deaf/hard
of hearing), or may not yet have enough exposure to English to make meaning out of another author's text. If such students can be guided to represent
their ideas in writing, they will have created a text that already makes sense
to read and reread. This allows learners to apply and solidify what they're
learning about written representations of English.

The same is true of people who know English, but are learning to read for
the first time as adults: writing and (re)reading their own texts ensures exposure to something that is meaningful and comprehensible.

In 1997, Victoria Purcell-Gates published a book that chronicled her
study of an Appalachian family caught in what she described as a cycle of
low literacy. The young children were struggling to learn to read, and their
parents struggled to help them because of their own struggles with literacy
and the consequentially small place of the printed word in their everyday
lives.

Purcell-Gates's approach involved tutoring both the children and their
mother, yet early readers with predictable texts are hardly designed to hold
the interest of adults. The mother was not prepared to read texts at the level
of her thinking and reasoning, so Purcell-Gates encouraged her to write for a
few minutes each day, to guess at the spellings she didn't know, and to read
back what she wrote.

Like students whose pathway to literacy involves writing first, she
learned spelling as patterned representation, instead of a series of rules. She
learned about authors' purpose and intention by being one herself. Even short
journal entries that are simply about the day or about a familiar task allow
readers to apply what they know about how written language works (often

from environmental print) to construct a message. They then have that message that already makes sense to them to read and reread.

For students who have already developed some reading skills, Graham and Hebert (2010) report that writing about what you read improves both reading and content knowledge. That is, students are more likely to understand and remember what they read if they are asked to write about it. In fact, multiple genres of writing have this effect—summarizing, responding, taking notes, and so forth because writing requires students to process what they have read in order to put it into their own words and record those words in a new modality (written instead of read or spoken).

When we just think about what we read, we may be hearing or visualizing words that add up to ideas, but when we're asked to write them—to pick the words that represent the ideas and pick the spelling patterns that make those words—we have morphed an intangible thought into a concrete form. We have not just read, but considered, written, and maybe even reread what we wrote.

Graham and Hebert further conclude that reading comprehension improvement is directly correlated with the amount of writing students do. They argue that this is because teaching students about sentence, paragraph, and text structure makes them more sensitive to and thoughtful about these things as readers. It seems that if you learn how to construct a word, sentence, paragraph, or story, you have also learned how to take one apart.

WHY WRITING TOOK A BACKSEAT TO READING, BUT SHOULDN'T HAVE

The de-emphasis on writing and writing instruction comes from two main sources. Both are national, both are unfortunate, and both have to do with money, not literacy. The first source is national trends in high-stakes testing. Writing is not as frequently tested and is therefore not as frequently taught.

One reason for this is that, unlike reading, there are few measures for writing achievement that are efficient and accepted as reliable and valid. We have accepted multiple-choice questions as indicators of reading comprehension though they merely *indicate* (rather than fully demonstrate) reading proficiency. The American public is relatively comfortable with this efficient manner of measuring reading, but has no such affinity (thank goodness) for short cuts to measuring writing.

Writing most often has to be scored by humans (or sometimes by oxymorons called "intelligent machines"), and evaluated based on a small number of writing samples (one or two), rather than tens or hundreds of individual questions. In other words, the assessment of writing is time consuming, man-power intensive, and expensive: all things the educational testing industry eschews.

The second reason that writing has so often been de-emphasized compared to reading may be that it was completely left out of the report of the National Reading Panel due to time constraints. When this federally appointed, authoritative body came out with recommendations for instruction, curricular materials, and teacher preparation, writing wasn't mentioned at all.

A year after the NRP report was popularized in summary form the Carnegie Corporation published a report on effective writing instruction called "Writing Next" (a companion to "Reading Next" with a focus on fourth through twelfth grades). But, unlike the report of the NRP, "Writing Next" had nothing near the backing or publicity power.

The NRP report and summary was managed by McGraw-Hill's consulting and publicity firm and was distributed for free in pamphlet, PDF and video form (with the glossy pamphlet and ten-minute video highlighting different, often contorted, findings than the 500-plus-page full report—for more on this see Garan, 2004). One the other hand "Writing Next" was commissioned by the Carnegie Corporation and came out as a slim, paper volume available in print or PDF with comparatively little fanfare.

One can only imagine that it was not taken up by publicists with the same fervor because writing instruction has not and never will be as large a publishing or testing market as reading. Plus, literacy programs and schedules for literacy instruction had already been designed based on the NRP's "five pillars" of reading instruction.

It is also possible that the idea that reading and writing are reciprocal has allowed teachers and administrators to feel comfortable investing in reading instruction instead of writing instruction. As educators continue to de-emphasize anything that isn't tested, there is less and less time for untested subjects like science and social studies, let alone the less tested aspects of language arts (writing).

States that do assess writing on high stakes tests almost always do so by eliciting writing samples via a writing prompt. So, students prepare for testing by practicing writing to prompts, rather than writing about something meaningful to them for an authentic purpose. As Guthrie (2002) has shown (see figure 2), only a small percentage (10 percent) of a student's test score has to do with the format of the test. The largest percentage of a student's score has to do with their general ability to communicate successfully and strategically in writing. So, as with reading, our writing instruction should prioritize aspects of writing instruction based on their relative contribution to test scores.

If this were true, teachers would only spend 10 percent of instructional time practicing writing to prompts, and only up to 10 weeks before a high stakes test. The rest of the time would be spent on guided instruction, strategies for writing, and motivation, all of which are best served by writing something meaningful for an authentic purpose.

Writing instruction can be particularly exciting because it involves an insider look at language in action. Word choice isn't important because it's in the state standards; it's important because changing even a single word (or its spelling) can *do* something: to meaning, to responses, and to the interpretation or emotion of a reader.

Likewise, punctuation isn't important because it's part of being correct, it also *does* something to the way a sentence is read, and the impact it can have. Format is likewise not a matter of correctness, but a matter of clarity (with convention comes clarity) and a signal that this piece of writing belongs with certain others in its field: that it is one among many lab reports, editorials, or acrostic poems and therefore evokes and is framed by other pieces like it.

Although reading and writing support each other, the benefit of adding writing to a reading program should not be underestimated. Indeed it can be transformative for students who struggle with traditional paths to literacy (letter to sound, sounds to words, words together, words to meaning) either because of past frustration, learning style, hearing impairment or other learning difference.

Instead of viewing writing as the inverse of reading, perhaps we should begin to view writing first, and reading next. Perhaps writing first (thought to word, word to representation) would accommodate those with persistent reading difficulties even after significant sound- or code-based intervention (e.g., Torgeson, 2000; Phillips, Hayward, & Norris, 2011).

THE CONS OF INTEGRATING WRITING INSTRUCTION (CAUTION: SARCASM AHEAD)

1. Students may learn to communicate what they think and feel to wide audiences.
2. Students may see themselves as authors in conversation with their history and their community.
3. Students may decide to write in formats (and genres) that we have never imagined and can't measure.
4. What students write might change our minds, their lives, and the world.

Sarcasm is used here to expose what are perhaps illogical but plausible fears about teaching students to be powerful writers.

One of the easiest ways to disempower people is to tell them either implicitly or explicitly that their writing isn't good or doesn't matter. As a reflection and product of the author's mind, writing can be an intensely personal and powerful tool.

If students become producers, rather than merely receivers, of texts, they might reveal truths, document experience or expression, make changes. In short: it could be dangerous. If we don't want to know the stories or read the messages our students are capable of writing about their worlds, their lives, or about us, fill-in-the-blank quizzes and grammar lessons are a good way to ensure those stories never come out.

If, on the other hand, we came to teach students to be more powerful and more free, we'd provide students with both reasons and time to write, even those who do not yet write in conventional ways. After all, ideas can be encoded in more than just letters or conventionally spelled words, and sometimes the choice of representation (as in poetry and art) is an accomplishment in itself.

To be clear, there are no cons to teaching writing. Time spent on writing develops powerful writers and supports reading development at every level.

WHAT IF THEY DON'T WANT TO WRITE?

It is not uncommon for people of all ages to claim they don't like writing or aren't any good at it. Given the kinds of opportunities to write outlined by the materials that make publishing companies the most money (disposable workbooks, worksheets, quizzes, formulaic paragraphs, etc.) it isn't any wonder so many of us leave school with no interest or confidence in our own compositions.

The principles of motivation to read (choice, purpose, confidence) are no different than those for writing. Choice in writing can come in many forms: topic, format, audience, length, modality (handwritten, typed, illustrated), and so forth. Indeed most of the Common Core State Standards for literary analysis involve the exploration of the impact of the choices writers make—so, what better way to learn about them than making them yourself?

Providing choice in what to write and/or in how to represent what you write can be an invitation to engage, but writing takes persistence. Motivation to write, like motivation to read, is increased when students have an authentic reason to write and choice of what to write about.

Authentic purposes for writing require writing to an audience and, when possible, seeing the writing delivered to that audience. Audience, not convention, becomes the reason to care that ideas are written in a way that makes sense, with spelling, grammar, and mechanics that make it easy for others to understand.

Like reading, writing instruction is often divided into isolated skills instruction in which things like spelling, grammar, and mechanics are drilled in isolation using contrived lists of words and sentences. Teaching grammar in isolation is not just unmotivating, it's actually empirically proven to be less effective than teaching grammar in context (Graham & Perin, 2007; Langer & Applebee, 1986).

Writing isn't about conventions, it's about ideas: finding them, communicating them, and preserving them. Spelling, grammar, and mechanics merely exist in service of these goals and should never, ever be taught as goals unto themselves. There's simply no purpose in isolating or divorcing such things from their meaning-making goals, and there is even less reason to learn or remember them. Just as all reading instruction can be wrapped in meaning making, all writing instruction can be wrapped in communication.

In order to focus all writing instruction on expressive communication students must always be writing to an audience for a purpose. Everything from a short journal entry or exit slip, to a letter, editorial, essay, report, or poem should be written with an audience in mind.

As often as possible the audience should be real, not imagined, and the writing should be delivered to that audience. In some cases this takes very little effort (students show teachers what they know by completing an exit slip) and in some cases it requires mailing, delivering, or presenting the piece to its intended audience.

The delivery of student writing to an audience is the motivator for persistence through revising and editing because the work will represent the student and their ideas to something that matters within and/or outside of school. Finally, students shouldn't (and often won't) just take our word for it that their writing can have an impact and will evoke responses. They should see it happen. They should know the power of their own words and the writing choices that work most powerfully for them.

Even when writing to communicate, instead of for contrived academic purposes, some students have built up years of reluctance and resistance around writing. As with reading, there may be limited identity resources for students to draw upon as they try to envision themselves as the kind of people who write.

Young students may think writing is only for girls or people with good handwriting. Older students may think writing is only associated with story writing or courses in the humanities. On the contrary, the National Survey of Student Engagement (2012) found that college seniors majoring in physical sciences wrote an average of 114 pages for school during their senior years. Their peers in the social sciences wrote an average of 171 pages.

Part of the solution here is simply myth-busting: people in *all* professions and all walks of life have reasons to write, and often must write in order to demonstrate their competence or disseminate their ideas, concerns, and wishes. Another part of the solution is honestly representing the kinds of writing that are useful outside of academic settings. For example:

- Almost nobody writes fill-in-the-blank sentences or formulaic paragraphs outside of school.
- Few people will write essays in the shape of hamburgers or answers in a study guide.
- Almost no one will ever write to a prompt, especially while a timer is running. Indeed consistently writing to a prompt in school may stunt the development of strategies to generate ideas for writing in the outside world and certainly stymies the potential power of topic choice to motivate writers. If these academic formats are useful as scaffolds or diagnostic tools for specific standards they should be used *with*, not in place of, more authentic formats and genres.

Another reason students may be reluctant to write, especially when it comes to longer compositions, is they have not yet had explicit instruction in writing. Writing is so often used in service of other kinds of learning (write this spelling word five times, fill in the blank for vocabulary words, list your observations of the plant, fill in the study guide for this chapter) that there is often little attention to writing as composition beyond essay structure and grammar.

Students need expert writers (their teachers) to model expert writing and thought processes. They need guided experiences constructing texts and making "writerly" choices, and they need the opportunity (and reason) to practice and experiment with writing. There are so many reasons to write in real life it seems silly to invent contrived assignments just for school. And it seems even sillier to assume students will intuit the thought processes required to write well in all the formats and genres they attempt.

WHAT YOU SHOULD SEE IN A CLASSROOM WITH A FOCUS ON WRITING

1. Every student has the opportunity to write something meaningful (in conventional or unconventional ways; long or short; rough draft or polished) every day.
2. All writing assignments (even short, quick writes) have an explicit purpose and audience—and time is spent delivering the writing to that audience in order to fulfill the purpose.

   a. Mailing letters, hosting publishing parties, or formatting a class book are not frivolous "Kodak moments": they are necessary acknowledgments of the integrity and importance of student writing. Administrators should provide support for such activities and should be there as an audience whenever possible. If students write to you, write back.

b. If writing is composed, graded, and then returned without reaching its intended audience, students get the message that their writing "isn't for real; it's for school," and therefore doesn't matter.

3. Writing assignments across settings and content areas reflect *real writing for real reasons* in terms of format, purpose, and style.

a. Students write in a wide variety of genres and formats for a variety of reasons, some of which are their own.

4. Writing assignments vary in length and involve *student composition*, rather than filling in blanks, formulas, or writing after a pattern or narrow prompt.

a. Students have the opportunity and responsibility to generate ideas, formulate them, and decide how they are best represented in text. When these choices are always made for them, motivation and learning are lost.

WAYS TO INVEST IN WRITING AS COMMUNICATION

1. Have students write interview questions that they can ask (other) adults in their lives in order to learn what kinds of writing they use at work and at home. Model assignments after these authentic formats and purposes for writing. Use them as touchstones when exploring more conventional academic formats.

2. Model possible thought processes behind every step of the writing process, and invite students to share their thinking as well. This will provide a bank of possible ways to approach writing for those who get "stuck."

a. When introducing a new format or genre, consider collaboratively writing something with the class so that students can watch and/or participate in each step of the process before writing independently.

3. Students should write about things that matter because it allows them to bring the relevant background knowledge and intrinsic motivation to the task.

a. Allow students to use things that inspire them to generate ideas for writing. These include art, music, current events, topics or activities of interest, and their academic lives.

4. Writing and the writing process take time. Plan to address multiple standards within several important writing assignments rather than many mini assignments with little time to revise, edit and publish the work.

POINTS FOR DISCUSSION

1. What are the purposes and audiences associated with the professional versions of the subject(s) you teach? How closely do your assignments mirror these?
2. If time for writing is not already built in to you class, where might you find time to invest in writing to an audience for a real purpose? Where in a unit of study would this make the most sense?
3. What would students need to know or see you do in order to be able to write well in your class? When/how might they learn the thought and writing processes that you know and use?

Chapter Six

Every Reader Talks with Peers about Reading and Writing

The role of student discourse is perhaps the most underestimated and underused element of classroom instruction in US public schools—especially at the secondary level.

WHY TALKING WITH PEERS ABOUT READING AND WRITING IS NON-NEGOTIABLE

It's powerful and it's free. Perhaps because it is free and is always already available, we seem to have long underestimated the impact of peer conversations and student talk about texts. In fact, several decades of research from K–12 grade and out of school settings suggests peer conversations have a measureable impact on comprehension, engagement, motivation, vocabulary, and language competence.

Achievement

In the late 1980s, Martin Nystrand and Adam Gamoran began publishing what would amount to a robust body of research on the importance of discussion in secondary English classrooms. Across middle and high school settings, they repeatedly reported that reciprocal interactions between teachers and students—that is, classroom conversations with open-ended questions in which teachers incorporate student responses into future questions—have a profound effect on engagement and achievement.

More recently, in 2006, Nystrand conducted a meta-analysis of research regarding the impact of discussion on achievement and concluded that the sum of available research strongly suggests that discussion boosts achievement. Furthermore, even limited amounts of discussion have a measurable and substantive impact. Nystrand reported that as little as 10 minutes a day of discussion was enough to boost engagement, motivation and achievement for students across settings and multiple studies.

He suggested that this is not only due to the motivation of engaging in conversation, or the accountability of being asked to speak, but the cognitive processing involved in formulating one's contributions to discussions. For example, in order to participate, students must consider a text-related concept, blend it with what they know, and formulate a response others will understand and react to.

As Malloy and Gambrell (2010) put it, "Discussion offers an opportunity to externalize thought and to co-construct meanings with others in a manner that builds knowledge and enlarges perspectives for all who participate" (p. 253). Discussion is not just answering questions; it is a combination of cognitive processes such as thinking, verbalizing, listening and observing, comparing, and rethinking, which, especially in combination, can lead to critical thinking and deeper learning (Malloy & Gambrell, 2010).

The learning theories that support the use of student conversations with peers and with teachers is grounded in the Vygotskian notion that cognitive abilities develop as a result of social interactions. Vygotsky's ideas have been translated as, "When one is required to explain, elaborate or defend one's position to others, as well as to oneself, striving for an explanation often makes a learner integrate and elaborate knowledge in new ways" (1978, p. 158). That is, participating in conversation is a way of engaging thinking that leads to learning.

Besides cognitive dimensions, conversations in classrooms also have important affective and sensory contributions to learning. All of the cognitive processes of conversation will also involve

> contextual traces that refer to the social event (seeing the faces and body language of the group members), the physical context of the discussion (how the classroom looks and sounds), the smells of cafeteria food wafting through the corridor, and the social and affective memories of the discussion, such as feelings of embarrassment or excitement or the emotional charge of a speaker's comment. (Malloy & Gambrell, 2010)

Thus conversation is not only important for cognition, but for memory, socioemotional development, and social relationships.

Unfortunately, in a study of over 100 eight and ninth grade classrooms, Nystrand and Gamoran also reported that whole classroom discussions averaged only fifty seconds per lesson in eighth grade and fifteen seconds per lesson in ninth grade (Nystrand and Gamoran, 1991). Far less than the modest amount of time needed for student discussion to make a positive impact.

In some ways, their studies of the presence of discussion in secondary classrooms took up where Cazden's 1988 book left off identifying the common patterns of interactions in elementary classrooms. Cazden and others explained that a striking majority of classroom interactions could be described by the IRE (initiate-respond-evaluate) or IRF (initiation-response-feedback) pattern. These patterns, though common, are considered less engaging and sometimes less effective because they do not allow students to freely construct responses (they are always answering a question with a known answer) and they stunt the unfolding of elaboration and discussion.

In some settings, the IRE (Mehan, 1979) pattern is so entrenched that it comes to encapsulate all that it means to sound like a teacher or play school. This "teacher-y" talk constantly uses the same prosody (ask questions . . . wait a beat for response . . . and evaluate the response with "good" "yes" or "anyone else?"). You know if you are falling into the familiar IRE pattern because you have to restart the conversation after every student response. For example:

Teacher: What's today?

Student: Tuesday.

Teacher: That's right, Tuesday . . . . And what's tomorrow?

Student: Wednesday.

The next conversational turn requires a new initiation by the teacher, not elaboration or response. Students are reciting known information rather than formulating their own responses—in other words, they are reciting rather than using language to learn. For example,

Teacher: The product of six and four is . . .

Students in unison: 24.

Teacher: Very good. Twenty-four. And what do we do when we finish our math work?

Students in unison: Put it in our desks.

Teacher: That's right, put it in our desks. And do we talk while we do that?

Students in unison: No.

Teacher: That's right. We quietly put things in our desks.

Though some considered this pattern a useful check for understanding, good practice, or rehearsal of knowledge, Nystrand and Gamoran have demonstrated that its opposite, reciprocal discussion, is strongly associated with both engagement and achievement. Meanwhile, recitation patterns are associated with control.

As Dudley-Marling and Paugh (2005) point out, "the rich get richer, and the poor get direct instruction" (p. 156). In other words, higher-achieving students whose teachers believe in their ability to construct knowledge allow them to talk and to lead discussions. Lower-achieving students whose teachers are not convinced students can respond well independently may be forced into a patterned system of call and choral response.

As Allington (2009) has noted, struggling readers and English language learners are perhaps the least likely of all students to be asked to talk about what they read. Instead, they are asked to prove that they read. Likewise, poor readers are assumed not to have understood, and are most often asked the simpler, closed-ended questions, rather than engaged in substantive discussion.

Open-ended and student-initiated discussions are a hallmark of gifted and talented classrooms (Netz, 2012) but are all but absent in lower-performing classrooms where scripted curricula are prescribed as interventions for low achievement. This is mostly because an IRE pattern is predictable, plan-able and controllable. If we do not believe students can think of their own correct answers, we teach them how to come out with our correct answers—to choose from a predetermined set of options in a predetermined, predictable pattern.

When it comes to student writing, the benefits of talk are perhaps even more obvious as students switch the modality of expression between written and spoken English. Though arguably similar, the benefit of talking about reading is somehow less obvious than that of revoicing ideas one has written.

Talking about one's own writing creates a social world around the text: people who know about it, people who could form its audience. Fall, Webb, and Chudowsky (2000) found that allowing students to talk about what they would write before writing reliably increased achievement across indicators. This could be because social incentive to clearly communicate initiated ideas and inspired students to formulate their thoughts in advance. It may also be that students were more comfortable or familiar with planning language to match their ideas orally than in writing.

It could also be that students are able to actively use oral language to learn language. They try out vocabulary and try on styles in conversation to see their interactional impact. They learn about language and how it works in all its forms (written and spoken) by trying it out aloud, and seeing the response. Or, by formulating a thought in one modality (writing) and then reinforcing it by switching to a different modality (talking, or vice versa). When it comes to new vocabulary, *using* the target words in multiple modalities (written, spoken, read) is the most efficient and "robust" form of vocabulary instruction known to researchers (Beck, McKeown, & Kucan, 2002).

WHY STUDENTS ARE RARELY ASKED TO TALK ABOUT WHAT THEY READ OR WRITE

In a 1998 study Commeyras and DeGroff found that 95 percent of teachers they surveyed value the idea of peer discussion of text, but only 33 percent reported actually using discussion in their classes. So why ignore what so many teachers and researchers believe to be an important and valuable practice?

We Worry They'll "Just Talk" (or Something Worse) Instead of Talking about Texts

Harvey Daniels, the father of literature circles, once famously said that literature circles in schools should be exactly like adult book groups in every way, except for the wine. In order for readers to look forward to talking with peers about what they read or write they will have to be allowed to "just talk" their way in and out of texts, related ideas, funny stories, current worries, and so forth. No one signs up for a weeknight activity that involves identifying the main character and summarizing. Conversations can and should wander a bit in order to be rich and meaningful.

The best way to ensure that literate conversations occur in their allotted time is to provide authentic reasons to talk about texts. In some cases open-ended discussion questions do just that. Assigning group roles (e.g., time-keeper, notetaker, focuser, presenter) can help students facilitate their own conversations around topics you choose. Even better, however, are discussions that center around real applications or uses of the text.

If students are reading and writing real texts for real reasons, there will be built-in real reasons to talk about them. If students write editorials to send to local newspapers, their peers are a test audience who can give feedback and pointers. If students have read news reports about an upcoming election, their peers are a debate team looking for evidence of bias in the text and searching for information to form an opinion.

If students have read a weather report, they might discuss what sort of clothes this means they will wear and which activities might be best for the day. If they've written personal narratives, since their goal is to share their stories with a real audience, their peers can tell them what parts of the story are most clear and compelling. The purpose for reading/writing becomes a reason for talking about texts.

Some countries have made a habit of using authentic discussions of text as a way to assess students without asking them to engage in contrived academic activities simply to prove their ability for authentic applications. For example, Peter Johnston (2005) described a multilayer assessment of literacy and literate conversations that is included as a test item in New Zealand's National Educational Monitoring Project. Instead of a passage with multiple guess questions at the end, this test item required students to act as a class library committee and work together evaluate a set of texts and provide justifications for those they would include in their library.

Whereas no one in the out-of-school world reads passages to answer multiple choices questions, adult readers frequently evaluate what they read to decide whether to buy it, share it, use it, keep it, or recommend it to others. As Johnston (2005) notes: "The activity requires the students to generate and negotiate evaluative criteria for the qualities of books, apply the criteria, take a position, argue persuasively, actively listen, and negotiate a group position" (p. 686). It also gives students something to talk about.

Allowing the "social" in social learning sometimes makes teachers nervous, and rightly so. Sometimes, leaving students to their own devices is followed by students saying or doing mean things. What's more, there is no product to point to at the end of the day to show how much "work" was "done" in conversation. Nevertheless, given the stakes, worries about classroom management are simply not a good enough reason to eliminate rich opportunities for learning. Similarly, the notion of productivity reinforced by piles of worksheets and checks on a spreadsheet have very little to do with the kind of learning literacy requires.

Still, it is important to have some measure of what works or is valuable about classroom talk. In most cases an informal comparison is enough to calm administrators and motivate students. For example, compare the quality (conceptual coherence, structure, detail, length, in that order) of students' written responses when asked to write directly after reading versus after first talking about what was read. You will likely find increased quality and engagement if conversation is a part of the equation.

Likewise, if you have discussions regarding independent reading, compare the scope and volume of texts readers choose when they get to discuss what they are reading with peers. Peer discussions about texts create reasons to read (so you have something to share), reasons to consider what was read (so you know what to say) and an opportunity to learn about texts you may want to read in the future.

Kelley and Clausen-Grace (2006) have demonstrated that allowing students time to talk about what they read increases both the volume and diversity of the texts they read on their own. This is a testament to the social motivation to read and choose specific texts. The relative benefit of building in opportunities to talk about texts could be documented by comparing reading logs with and without conversation time, or surveying student reading habits before and after periods where they regularly had time to talk about what they read.

Talking with adults and other older role models has a similar social benefit. It provides a reason to read, a purpose for knowing about what you read. It also demonstrates that reading can be social and is important enough that adults want to talk about it. Even adults who do not have the opportunity to read with their children can support their child's reading habits by talking with them about texts they've read and sharing how adults think about texts in their own lives.

It Takes Time

Compared to other strategies that have been used to influence comprehension, motivation, achievement, vocabulary, and language development, talking in class doesn't take much. It requires no materials, minimal preparation and only a few guidelines. You can transition to and from opportunities for talk relatively seamlessly and, unlike reading, students don't need to log hours of practice to benefit from it. Ten minutes a day is enough to make a measureable difference in engagement and achievement.

Compare the time it takes for a brief "turn and talk" or even a small group discussion to the time required to approach any one of the following: comprehension, motivation to read, reading engagement, vocabulary growth, language development, speaking and listening skills. Count up the money you'll save by investing in talk and invest it in texts of your students' choosing. Count up the time you've saved and use it for any non-negotiable. Examine the effort you've saved and give yourself the afternoon off!

We Think What We Have to Say Is More Important

Keep in mind that opportunities to talk are not just about spreading information or opinions. Rather the process of formulating oral discourse about a text is a way of learning in itself. If we do all the talking, we are depriving students of a powerful opportunity to learn and remember what we are so busy talking about.

Students who are too shy to speak up in class, or just slightly slower to come up with what they'd like to say, compared to all the Johnny-jump-ups with their hands in the air, still deserve the opportunity to put their literate thoughts into words. Allocating time and space for this may mean the difference between passive and active participation in literate thought.

They Haven't Read or Written Anything to Talk About

A final reason that students don't get to talk about their reading or writing in school is that they haven't done much of either one. If this is the case, see chapters 1–7.

WHAT YOU SHOULD SEE IN A CLASSROOM WHERE EVERY READER TALKS WITH A PEER ABOUT READING AND WRITING

1. Time is allocated for students to talk and there is a common understanding of the purpose of this time.
2. Teachers listen to students talk in large and small groups. If they participate, their interactions reformulate and/or elaborate (acknowledge) what students have said rather than solely evaluating it.
3. Students know quick and equitable ways to find and communicate with talking partners so that they talk to a range of classmates in respectful ways.
4. Students read and write things they want to talk about. When asked, they will talk with you about them.
5. Teachers model "literate conversations" by thinking aloud, providing conversation prompts, and/or providing students with specific group roles.

POINTS FOR DISCUSSION

1. Which aspects of the "cycle of reading success" are addressed when students talk with peers about their reading? What about when they talk with peers about their writing?
2. In classes where there is no time for students to talk about their reading/writing what takes its place? What is the value of that replacement?
3. Think of a text that your students have recently written or read. Why might someone read or write such a thing outside of a school setting? How and why might they talk about the text outside of school?

Chapter Seven

Every Reader Listens to a Fluent Reader Read Aloud

Parents and elementary school teachers are often told that "the single most important activity for building success in reading is reading aloud to children" (Anderson et al., 1985). They are perhaps less likely to be told another recommendation from the same source (Report of the Commission on Reading), that reading aloud "is a practice that should continue throughout the grades" (p. 51).

In the wake of the relative success of numerous efforts to raise awareness about the importance of reading aloud to young children, we must not forget these benefits can extend to older children in several important ways.

WHY LISTENING TO A FLUENT READER IS A NON-NEGOTIABLE

In 2000, Jacobs, Morrison, and Swinyard surveyed almost 2,000 elementary and middle school teachers and asked them to report how often they had read aloud to their students in the last ten days. As you might imagine, they found that as grade level increased, the frequency of planned read-alouds decreased. Kindergarten and first grade teachers reported reading aloud to their students an average of five times, while fifth and sixth grade teachers reported reading aloud an average of three times in the last ten days. Contrary to this trend in practice, there is no evidence that the efficacy of reading aloud to students diminishes with their age, reading ability, or the presence of disability labels (Hudson & Test, 2011).

Research on reading aloud in kindergarten through eighth grade provides strong evidence of the importance of reading aloud for language development, phonological awareness, print concepts, comprehension, and vocabulary (Swanson et al., 2011), and there is similar evidence that reading aloud in high school continues to have a powerful impact on vocabulary, comprehension, and engagement.

Read-alouds are perhaps even more important in the high school content area learning (in science, math, social studies, art, music) because they can explicitly and efficiently support every component of the cycle of reading success with discipline-specific texts:

1. They provide repeated, contextualized auditory exposure to content-specific **vocabulary** and the discourses of each content area (the mathematical register, scientific discourses, etc.).
2. They provide strong models of **fluency** that help students set an appropriate pace for reading a content-specific text.
3. They allow teachers to carry the burdens of word recognition and fluency while students concentrate on **comprehension**.
4. They build **engagement** by providing students with access to texts and ideas they may not be able to read about on their own because of access, time, or text difficulty.
5. They increase **confidence** for specific texts by showing students how a confident reader approaches and makes sense of them.
6. They provide a model of expert **decoding**, which allows students to attach an auditory memory of what a word should sound like (perhaps a word they have heard, but not yet read) to its printed representation.

The positive impact of reading aloud to students is not limited to the physical fact of auditory input. Researchers in the area of deafness posit that the opportunity to negotiate meaning between two languages (e.g., English and American Sign Language and/or a synthetic communication system) provides an opportunity for language to mediate learning (Vygotsky, 1978) and for social relationships to form the foundation of engagement and confidence in reading (Bandura, 1986; Schleper, 1997; Gallaudet Research Center, 2010).

Similarly, studies of English language learners support the use of read-alouds in both languages at home and at school because of the opportunity for language- and socially mediated learning (Thornburg, 1993). When teachers and parents have enough linguistic knowledge to be explicit about how they move between languages, read-alouds are also a time to build metalinguistic awareness. Students learn how an idea is expressed in each language, can use this comparison to infer something about the structure of each language, and can use one language to support their learning of another.

Thus, in some ways it may be helpful to think of listening to a fluent reader or reading aloud as an opportunity for students to be apprenticed to the cognitive processes of reading (Collings, Brown, & Holum, 1991) as well as the sociocultural norms and discourses of academic disciplines. Reading aloud provides a context for students and teachers to talk about text, language, and meaning making in real time.

Whether students are learning English for the first time, or learning the language of scientific, mathematical, or historical discourse in a secondary content area course, they need explicit models of how to read and make sense of texts in the target language. Since reading is a largely invisible activity, reading aloud, often while stopping to explain what you think as you read, is the clearest way to model literacy practices.

BAD MODELS AND SUPER MODELS

Frager (2010) has argued against reading aloud at the secondary level altogether for these reasons: it promotes student passivity, implies that reading happens in a linear (rather than recursive) way, and implies that there is only one possible interpretation of the text.

This is certainly a concern in settings where students are positioned as receptacles for auditory input, and a good reminder of two important principles of reading aloud:

1. There's a difference between hearing and *listening* (one active, one passive).
2. This difference parallels the difference between teachers reading aloud and thinking aloud while reading.

In order to encourage active listening with understanding (rather than passively hearing a bunch of words), all read-alouds need two elements:

1. A stated purpose for reading.
2. Some activation of relevant topic or background knowledge.

These two elements allow students to co-construct a reason to pay attention and set them up to understand. No adult routinely reads texts without background knowledge or without a reason for reading, so we should not expect children to listen that way. If we want active listening rather than passive hearing, we have to tell students what they should be listening for and why.

Beginning a read-aloud without activating prior knowledge is like leading students into a movie theater twenty minutes into the movie: they spend the first five minutes trying to figure out what's going on (and maybe losing interest) instead of beginning to spin a thread of meaning.

Likewise providing or co-constructing a goal for reading/listening (listen for the part where . . . ; listen to see if. . . ; watch how the author. . . ; raise your hand when you hear. . . ; see if you notice when . . .) involves considering the purpose of the text: what it can be used to do and what students will learn from it.

Exposure to oral language has the potential to build vocabulary and provide a model of fluency, and this potential is more likely to be actualized if students know what they're listening to and why. Still, vocabulary and fluency may not be the limiting factors for all students' reading development. Instead, it is likely that many students, especially students in upper grades, are most in need of support for comprehension strategies that go with the wide range of text types and formats they encounter across subjects.

If this is the case, students need a model of reading as thinking, not as recitation. And they need access to fluent readers' processes for reading: demonstrations that reading can be recursive, that word recognition involves problem solving, and that meaning is negotiated (not just identified).

As Beck and McKeown (2001) have demonstrated, read-alouds are even more effective when teachers stop to talk with students about the text as they go. In this way read-alouds are not merely language exposure, but can be comprehension instruction as well. Indeed, if students never have access to the thought processes that go along with comprehending texts across genres, topics, and formats, they have never had access to explicit comprehension instruction.

WHY READ ALOUD WHEN STUDENTS CAN READ?

Even students who can independently read all the words of their academic texts will benefit from read-alouds that offer exposure to an expert reader's thinking. This is true for two main reasons:

First, as Moje (2008) has noted, each of the academic disciplines can be viewed as a community of practice—students can learn each discipline (science, mathematics, social studies, language arts, etc.) by observing members of that community (their teachers) at work and slowly participating in the processes that sustain that work. This is how professional learning often happens outside of school settings and how it happened for the thousands of years before public school (Lave & Wenger, 2001).

"Practicing" a discipline in front of students means actually engaging in the everyday tasks, applications, and experiences of being a reader, writer, scientist, mathematician, linguist, and so forth. It requires *showing* and explaining the reading/thinking processes that go along with the texts used in the practice of each discipline:

1. How you approach a text:

    a. What you look at first
    b. What you do before reading
    c. How to set a purpose for reading and get ready to understand

2. How you think through a text:

    a. What you do as you read
    b. What you notice and pay close attention to
    c. How you know which parts are most important

3. What you do when you're done reading:

    a. What purpose the text serves
    b. How you record or organize your thoughts

Students need to see a model of the invisible processes that teachers—as expert readers and experts in their disciplines—use to read and make sense of a text. Reading a math textbook requires a different process than reading a newspaper article, a set of procedures, primary source documents, or a novel. These differences are grounded in the format and discipline-specific purposes for each text (e.g., to direct actions, to convey emotion, to argue a proof).

Second, if we never show students *how* we—as readers, experts, and mature language users—read, they will come away from the time with us with the implicit lesson that there is nothing to it; that it should be equally automatic and easy for them. When it isn't easy, the logical conclusion is that there is something wrong with them, or that they simply are not the same type of person (e.g., a reader, a math person, a science type) as we are.

Students may leave math, science, and sometimes even English classes believing (because they have no evidence to the contrary) that understanding texts in that class is a matter of magic or luck—that some students are good at it and some students are not. They may think they're just not a science type or an art person simply because they were never adequately apprenticed into the practice of making meaning from texts in that area.

As Alvermann (2003) has suggested, the "crisis" of adolescent literacy (Council on Advancing Adolescent Literacy, 2009) may not be a crisis of literacy as much as a crisis of the kinds of litera*cies* required in school. Students often have rich and varied "literate lives" outside of school, and still demonstrate difficulty with academic reading. They read lots of texts with purpose and fluency, but these are not the kinds of texts they see in class.

Alvermann suggests that such difficulty often has less to do with basic reading skills and more to do with the ability to make meaning from the increasingly wide variety of texts and reasons for reading that students encounter in middle and high school. For this, students need a model of an expert's approach to the texts that are used within each discipline's community of practice.

For example, as an educator you may not have a lot of experience or interest in reading legal documents. In fact, you probably only read them when you have to because they matter for your work, your political interests, or your rights. Even though you approach these texts with a purpose, you are not as practiced at reading them as someone who is frequently involved in law as a practice or a discipline. Lawyers and law professors, on the other hand, have strategies specific to these types of materials as well as a detailed understanding of the purpose and function that underlies their format and content.

Those involved in the practice of law may think of these strategies as tricks, tips, or approaches more than "strategies," because they were developed out of pragmatism, not for the purpose of instruction. Still, people who work with legal documents on a daily basis know what to look for, what to skim, where to turn first, what to keep track of, and so forth.

If a lawyer were to hold a legal document and read aloud from it as they read it to themselves (rather than as you might read it, starting at the top and going from left to right without skipping a single word), you would get a sense of their process: how they use text features and organization patterns to help them identify important phrases, and how they make a complex text make sense. If they were to pause and tell you what they were looking for, why and how they proceed, you would have an even clearer sense.

Similarly farmers, veterinarians, and agriculture education teachers know exactly how to approach reading the nutrition labels on animal feed. If a lawyer were to approach such a label, they might not know which text features or words to pay most attention to. If, however, they had some background knowledge about feed and animal nutrition requirements, they might know which lines of the "nutrition facts" chart to start with and which to look out for to avoid poisoning or compromising an animal. They might know what vitamins or supplements should be most valued, and which are just there as filler.

They might also know that you do not read a feed label straight down from top to bottom: you look for a few key elements and compare what you see on the label to what you know is most important for an animal's health and performance. For example, they might know that it is important to pay attention to the ratio of crude protein and energy on nutrition labels for horse feed. They would know that crude protein is written as a percent and can be found in roughly the same location on most labels. They would know that any feed with copper in it should not be fed to sheep, and they would know where copper is likely to be listed if it is included.

All of that knowledge about the content and organization of specific texts is usually hidden from students unless teachers explicitly point it out to them by modeling how they read and think about text. In this way, thinking aloud about how you understand specific texts may be the most powerful comprehension instruction available.

READ-ALOUDS/THINK-ALOUDS AS
COMPREHENSION INSTRUCTION

Many of us do not remember ever being told how to approach a primary source document in stages, that it isn't cheating to read a science textbook chapter backwards (from discussion questions to summaries to the introduction), or that reading in math automatically implies rereading, determining importance, and ignoring extraneous information. Many of us do not remember initially learning to read either, but that doesn't mean students don't need us to teach it.

Reading comprehension instruction at the secondary level is too often instruction free with teachers stuck in an assign-assess cycle of assigning readings, asking questions about them, and maybe going over the questions if students get them wrong. Difficulty with comprehension is too often met with unhelpful, blanket phrases like "read it again," "think about it" or worse: "think harder."

Like other unhelpful blanket phrases "think harder" carries no concrete meaning, but it implies that students aren't thinking or trying when they are confused. Students then have two choices: to believe this about themselves whether it was true or not or to lose trust in their teachers for assuming the worst about their efforts.

Reading comprehension strategies, sometimes called metacognitive strategies, provide a way of talking about thinking while reading that's more specific than "I read it . . . Now I get it." The commonly published list of comprehension strategies are simply more specific terms for the kinds of thinking it takes to make a text make sense. They are the actions of "active" reading, but they do not represent an end in themselves.

When researchers observed and interviewed strong readers in order to catalogue their meaning-making strategies, they noted specific kinds of thinking such as: making predictions, inferences, and connections; determining importance; clarifying; questioning; and keeping track of what is known.

They also noted that successful readers set purposes for reading, looked over a text before reading and constantly made decisions about what to read closely, quickly, or over again (Duke & Pearson, 2002).

They result of these and other studies is some version of the following "strategies" that have been repeated, reprinted and plastered on classrooms walls for more than a decade. Yet, more than knowledge of these terms, students need access to our ways of thinking and making sense of text—whether or not they fall neatly into a poster's list of categories.

You may notice that the terms just mentioned sound a lot like the scientific method, elements of mathematical thinking, and a historical inquiry process. In fact scientists, for example, may find it easier to rename certain strategies to fit scientific discourses. For example, they might describe their thought process as "creating a mental picture" rather than "visualizing" or "hypothesis checking" rather than "clarifying."

The terms themselves are not important; their specificity is. They help teachers make their invisible thought process visible to students by describing it. They provide a common vocabulary for thinking and talking about what we do while we read in order to make a text make sense. This is the instruction that is too often missing in an assign-assess cycle: an explanation of the way expert readers make a text make sense.

Table 7.1.   Reading Strategies

Predict	*In the future I think . . .* *Based on ____ I think . . .* *I think ____ will . . .*
Connect	*This reminds me of . . .* *This is just like . . .* *I can connect to this because . . .*
Infer	*I can tell that . . .* *I bet that . . .* *So far I think that . . .*
Visualize	*I can picture . . .* *From this I can see . . .* *____ probably looks like . . .*
Question/clarify	*I wonder why . . .* *I wonder if . . .* *It's confusing that . . .*
Evaluate	*In my opinion . . .* *I would rate this . . .* *I think the author is . . .*

Adapted from Duke and Pearson (2002).

WHAT YOU SHOULD SEE IN A CLASSROOM WHERE EVERY LEARNER LISTENS TO A FLUENT READER READ ALOUD

1. Strong readers (teachers and students) read aloud *and* all readers discuss meanings and implications of what was read.
2. Teachers model their own thinking as they approach, read, and make sense of the texts they assign.

    a. This might be as little as reading and talking about the first two sentences of an assignment sheet or the first paragraph of a chapter before assigning the rest to be read independently.

3. Students are not forced to read aloud or to read aloud in a preset sequence.

    a. Teachers often find that "round robin reading" (where students take turns reading in a circle or down a row) makes students spend more time looking ahead and rehearsing their part, or managing their anxiety, than following along and making meaning of what their peers read. "Popcorn reading" where a teacher calls on students to read at random alleviates the problem of following along, but increases anxiety about being called on without preparation. Voluntary reading alleviates both problems.

4. Students are aware of why they are reading what they are reading and can articulate an approach that matches their purpose (reading to figure out___; reading to find___; reading to observe how the author___).

POINTS FOR DISCUSSION

1. Students need access to models of the process, not just the outcome, of reading, especially when reading texts in new formats, genres or disciplines. How often do and should teachers in your grade use a read-aloud/think-aloud?
2. Where in your class period or an instructional cycle might it makes sense to incorporate read-alouds/think-alouds?
3. Who else besides teachers might be able to demonstrate their reading processes to students?
4. If transparency is important for demonstrating the "how" of comprehension, what kinds of practice might help teachers become keenly

aware of the kinds of thinking they use to make texts make sense to them?

5. Are you aware of how you think when you read? If not, show a text you often use in class to someone who routinely looks at other types of text. Notice what they look at first, what they pay most attention to and where they get confused or interpret differently than you do.

Chapter Eight

Wanted: Instruction Wrapped in Meaning, Grounded in Purpose

Readers will read when they have something they can and want to read. Reading (and writing) is developed by reading (and writing). For some students, it might be better to say that writing (and reading) is developed by writing (and reading) as the emphasis on one form or another may not serve all learners equally well. Still, as simple as it may seem, even good intentions can go awry when it comes to planning and executing effective literacy instruction.

The most effective literacy instruction is layered with reasons to read, opportunities to choose, purposes for writing, people to read with, and audiences to write to. Where any one of these things is missing, the glue that binds all component skills together—a combination of motivation, interest, and confidence—may also be missing.

This chapter contains two sets of possible "days in the life" of readers who interact with literacy instruction that is layered with all the non-negotiables: wrapped in meaning and grounded in purpose. They are some of many possibilities for meaning-driven instruction that maximizes instructional time for literacy, and organizes common routines around the non-negotiables described in this book.

The danger in describing only two examples is it may seem to promote a single version of what counts as typical or ideal. The argument of this book has been that there is no such thing. Still, principles without examples are not always useful to those engaged in the everyday work of teaching and learning. So, please consider these examples as only two of many, many possible versions of typical and meaning-driven instruction.

Each described activity is based on real observations of real classroom practices from classrooms across the country. They are not perfect or singular in nature. Rather they are meant to illustrate how similar structures in a school day can be used to kink the cycle of reading success or to support all aspects of it over and over again. Each period of the day is presented side-by-side for easy comparison and annotated (in bold) with an analysis of some of the opportunities for literacy each affords.

TWO DAYS IN THE LIFE

The difference between typical and meaning-driven instruction centers around the actualization of two principles:

1. All reading and writing has purpose.
2. Component skills are practiced in the context or service of meaning making.

These two principles make way for all other non-negotiables, but they do not guarantee them. In order for students to have balanced and effective literacy instruction each instructional event is layered with opportunities to use, practice, extend and integrate skills, strategies, reasons, and formats for reading and writing.

The schedule described in the meaning-driven column in table 8.1 could include allocations of *up to*:

- Sixty minutes of independent reading
- Forty-five minutes of reading instruction (shared reading or modeling)
- Thirty additional minutes of reading instruction for students who are struggling
- Eighty minutes of writing
- Thirty minutes of talking with peers about reading or writing.
- A total of more than four hours of literacy learning opportunities per school day

Given that more than half of this allocated time for reading/reading instruction involves is choice reading at or near the student's independent level, the ratio of allocated to actual time spent reading should be relatively high.

In addition, given that time for student writing assignments involves a teacher model, a clear purpose, audience, and chance to share the finished product, the ratio of allocated to actual time spent writing should be relatively high.

Typical

Meaning-Driven

8:00–8:15 Settle in time: Students are allowed into the classroom as buses continue to arrive.

Students have a folder of "morning work," low-level worksheets that students can complete easily without needing help—and can complete these to earn points. Those that complete many sheets often earn prizes; those that don't, never do.

- Up to 15 min competitive, low-level activities

Morning stations allow students to illustrate scenes from yesterday's read-aloud, build words with magnetic letter tiles, make observations of the frog tank, or read in the corner library. Students can choose to share their work at the end of the day if they are particularly proud of what they did.

- Up to 15 min independent choice reading or writing

8:15–8:30 Morning meeting

Announcements are read to students. The teacher asks students questions about weather and calendar information for the day. Then, they go over the day's schedule as posted.

- Up to 15 min of checks for understanding of calendar and weather knowledge

Announcements, along with the day's date and schedule are posted in the form of a message to students. Important announcements are reread chorally and/or by volunteers—sometimes in various voices for entertainment or emphasis. The teacher asks the students to notice letter patterns in the message that are new or that she/he finds students are using, but confusing. Students volunteer to read, point to, or add corrections to the morning message so that it makes sense to all readers.

- Up to 15 min shared reading, fluency practice (repeated readings) and contextualized decoding instruction

8:30–8:50 Read-aloud

The teacher reads aloud and stops to ask students questions in order to make sure they are paying attention. They ask comprehension and vocabulary questions after the story to check for understanding.

- Up to 20 min of fluency building by listening to a strong model

The teacher reads aloud while stopping to share her thinking, and inviting students to share their thinking (think-aloud) with a partner or by raising their hand at predetermined points in the text—students can also share their responses, guesses and questions. Each time the teacher purposefully chooses meaning-making strategies to highlight and name for the students.

- Up to 20 min of fluency and comprehension building by listening to a strong model think aloud

8:50–9:20 Reading

Students rotate through centers that include reading in the library, listening to a book on tape, playing a vocabulary matching game, reading tongue twisters repeatedly for fluency. Once a week students from a higher grade come to read with these students.

- Up to 7 min of fluency practice
- 7 min of independent choice reading

9:20–10:00 Writing

Small groups of students rotate through centers that include: handwriting practice, spelling word flash cards, sight word word-searches and writing templates that guide students to write three details "about my day."

- Up to 10 min penmanship development

Students go directly from the read-aloud to independent reading of a text they select from their browsing boxes. Their task is to read their own text and use the strategy just highlighted in the read-aloud. After 20 minutes, students transition to rotating through centers which may include: independent reading; word work; partner reading (of two-voice poems or short scripts for repetition); reading along with a recording, guided reading with the teacher; recording a book on tape for a younger reader (students can do this once they have read, reread and mastered fluency with a text of their choice).
Once a week students from a higher grade come to read with these students. Students may use their independent reading time to choose and practice a text they want to read to their buddy.

- Up to 20 independent choice reading
- Up to 10 min reading or skills practice

The teacher begins the period by demonstrating a strategy for one aspect of the writing process on her own sample, then checks for understanding of this strategy by inviting students to do the same to a class text. Students then create their own text, written to an audience of their choice, by rotating through centers that represent each stage of the writing process. Each stage is supported by visual scaffolds (spelling, format and organization windows) and relevant materials (draft paper, mentor texts, a purpose

10:00–10:15 Snack, break, bathroom

Students line up to go to the bathroom/water fountain. Some bring books with them to read in the hall.

- Up to 10 min of optional independent reading

Students talk with a partner about what they wrote during snack time (like one might in a coffeehouse). They report (oral or written) what their partner told them at the end of the break. Students take turns going to the bathroom using a list the students generated by combining their name word wall with a math lesson on sequencing and frequency.

- Up to 15 min of peer conversations about writing

10:15–11:00 Math

Students begin with "minute math" worksheets to practice automatic math facts. The teacher demonstrates a new operation, shows students where words associated with it are on the word wall, and then students practice it in their workbooks. The teacher circulates to provide extra support where needed.

- Instruction that would support matching new vocabulary to a definition
- Up to 30 min of math skills practice

Students begin with "minute math" worksheets to practice automatic math facts. The teacher describes a class problem or project and students brainstorm how they could use their math facts to solve it. The teacher has chosen a problem that can be solved using a certain operation or procedure and introduces this as an efficient answer to the shared problem. The students nominate someone to create a word-wall card for the new words associated with this task, and they decide where the card should be placed among existing math words on the wall. Students work in small groups to write and illustrate a description of how they solved the problem together before breaking into pairs to practice the operation on other examples.

- Instruction that supports a conceptual understanding of vocabulary
- Up to 10 min of writing about math using math terms to demonstrate understanding

11:00–11:45 Science or social studies (rotates)

The teacher provides a list of definitions for a new concept in science. Students take turns reading aloud from a grade-level textbook about a concept in science. If there is time, students watch or engage with a demonstration of the concept.

- Instruction that would support matching new vocabulary to a definition
- Up to 30 min of shared reading without instruction or modeling

The teacher describes new vocabulary by using it to demonstrate a new science concept live or via video. Definitions are offered as the words are encountered. At the end of the demonstration, students create word wall cards for the new words and place them on the wall. Having previewed the topic and vocabulary, the teacher models how a scientist would read the first section of their textbook on the topic, pointing out the process and strategies of making a textbook make sense. Then students finish the textbook section in small groups or on their own. If there is time, students watch or engage with another demonstration of the concept.

- Instruction that supports a conceptual understanding of vocabulary
- Up to 5 min of a strong model for content area reading
- Up to 10 min shared/independent reading of a science text

11:45–12:45 Lunch and recess

(Lunch, recess)

A small handful who struggle with reading have come in with an "after lunch bunch" for guided reading, 1:1 instruction and/or more independent reading.

- Up to 30 min targeted individualized instruction

12:45–1:45 Special classes

Special area teachers give students content-related worksheets and vocabulary quizzes. They use and define content-specific words in class.

- Instruction that would support matching new vocabulary to a

Special area teachers teach, use and post their specialized vocabulary and ways of representing ideas (art, charts/graphs, notation). By using and showing the literacies that go along with each, they allow students to participate in each discipline by learning the oral/written language that goes with it.

- A model of content-specific literacy strategies

1:45–2:45 Project time (social studies and/or science integration)

Students fill in worksheets that ask them to summarize their science experiment and then use the vocabulary in a word search. Students who finish early can use the vocabulary in a crossword puzzle.

- Up to 1 hour practice matching new vocabulary to a definition and filling in forms

Teachers describe examples of different genres scientists use to communicate their research findings. Students can then choose to write: an entry in their "lab notebooks" that will be shared and compared among peers, or write a newspaper style report on the day's events to show someone at home. Teachers evaluate these for consistency with the genre/format; sequencing of information; level of description; match to the described examples.

- Up to 20 min writing modeling
- Up to 40 min practice discipline-specific writing for a purpose to an audience

2:45–3:00 Read-aloud/share-aloud

Students sit in a large circle and take turns with 'show and tell' objects from home. Teachers may also use this time to continue a read-aloud or catch up on an unfinished quiz or assignment from earlier in the day.

- Classroom catch-up or
- Up to 15 min social skill development in the context of describing possessions

In large or small groups students decide on one thing to share from their work that day/week that they are proud of. Teachers use this time to highlight efforts and strong examples of different skills. They may instead use the time to continue the morning's read-aloud.

- Up to 15 min social skill development in the context of reading/writing/talking
- Reinforces purpose and audience

3:00–3:15 Begin bus loading

Students are told they can read quietly at their desks or start their homework. Most start their homework as the only book at their desk contains few pages they can read independently.

Students are told they can read something from their browsing box of leveled options and/or write a recommendation for a book they have finished. Recommendations are posted on the wall

• Up to 15 min independent reading of a grade-level text	near the library for other students to review. • Up to 15 min independent choice reading

Table 8.2. A Day in the Life in Secondary School (grades 6–12)

8:15–8:30: Homeroom

Loudspeaker announcements and students can read, chat or work on homework. • Study hall	Loudspeaker announcements and students can listen to, read or discuss current events described in available newspapers, magazines, and websites. • Up to 15 min of independent reading or text-based discussion

8:40–9:30: English

Students take turns reading from the Shakespeare play in their literature anthology. They take a vocabulary quiz at the end of the period and create flashcards for a quiz on the plot of the play. Students read the next scene for homework and summarize it. • Up to 50 min shared reading without repetition or a strong model	Small groups of students rehearse and then perform individual scenes. Then, as would an illustrator, play or movie director, groups add these scenes to visual storyboards of events and decide which are most important and which could be eliminated in their own versions of the production. Students read 20 minutes worth of a text of their choice for homework and write two Post-it-note style responses (brief questions or thoughts) as they read. • Up to 25 min shared reading, fluency practice • Up to 25 min literary analysis and representation

9:40–10:30: Science

Students fill out a study guide by taking notes on a PowerPoint lecture designed to help them review before a test. • Up to 50 mins practice filling in forms	Students divide up sections of the chapter related to the current unit; identify the most important information, images and processes in their section and present these to the class in a format of their choice (poster, handout, PowerPoint slide, skit) in order to review for a test. • Up to 50 mins determining importance and representing information

10:40–11:30 Elective: for example, agriculture, health, or shop class

The teacher hands out directions that have been rewritten to be as simple and clear as possible, then verbally explains a project. Students follow directions and ask for help when needed.

- Up to 50 min practice following written directions when supported by oral repetition

The teacher demonstrates how they approach directions in the format most often used in their fields (blueprints, nutrition labels, soil sample reports, etc.); students then use the content-specific text to construct a model or describe the course of action it should inspire.

- Up to 10 min comprehension instruction via teacher modeling
- Up to 35 min interpreting content-specific texts

11:40–12:20 lunch and club meetings

The environmental club prints pre-made posters about recycling and posts them around the school

- Up to 20 min practice following oral directions

The environmental club meets to design and review potential poster designs. Students select the designs with the most potential impact and information to post around the school

- Up to 20 min evaluation and discussion about purpose, message and audience

12:30–1:20 Math

Students go over the homework with the teacher. In preparation for an upcoming test, students complete practice problems in groups.

- Up to 50 min using oral language to communicate mathematical ideas

Students check homework and identify problems for discussion based on the frequency of errors. When a problem requires discussion, students divide into groups to come up with a written explanation of what they know about the problem and how to solve it. Groups present these to the whole class and each group takes questions on their process and answer.

- Up to 50 min discussing and using oral and written language to communicate mathematical ideas

1:20–2:10 Foreign language

Students all read the same passage from their textbook in order to fill out a study guide of facts about a country in which their

Groups of students each have a set of texts of various genres on the same topic. They divide up these magazines, brochures, target language is used.

Then, they create, illustrate and practice using vocabulary flash cards or foldables to memorize new words.

- Up to 25 min shared reading
- Up to 24 min definition memorization

2:20–3:10 Social studies

The teacher provides a list of vocabulary words and their definitions before students take turns reading a chapter about creation myths from different cultures.

- Up to 50 min shared reading without instruction or a strong model

travel guides, websites and news articles to collect information about a country in which their target language is used for a future project. Then students read, rehearse and perform short skits that incorporate their vocabulary words.

- Up to 25 min independent choice reading
- Up to 25 min fluency practice

A teacher reads or shows (video) a creation myth and demonstrates his/her thought process for analyzing what it says about the culture, what questions she has about it, and what it is similar to. Students then work in groups to analyze more examples in a similar way.

- Up to 15 min strong model of comprehension and fluency
- Up to 35 min shared reading for a purpose

Given the same schedule and activity structure in table 8.1, the typical classroom could include allocations of up to

- Thirty-two minutes of independent reading
- Forty-seven minutes of reading instruction (shared reading or strong fluency model)
- Zero additional minutes of reading instruction for students who are struggling
- Zero minutes of writing to an audience with a purpose
- Zero minutes of talking with peers about reading or writing
- Less than an hour and a half of literacy learning opportunities per school day

Multiply these approximate numbers across a week and over a year and we can imagine how it is that some students fall and stay behind. Similarly, look for the presence of the non-negotiables in these classrooms and note that even though both rooms do some of them sometimes, the meaning-driven classroom does them more and often together. This integration makes literacy (and other) instruction far more powerful.

A similar comparison can be made between the typical and ideal day in the life of students in the upper grades (see table 8.2).

Nowhere on this secondary school schedule is there a content area class that has been supplanted by an English course, or content that has been supplanted by reading instruction. Rather the reading that goes along with fully participating in each discipline's area of study is demonstrated and used in the course of regular instruction.

Even though only one course is explicitly designated for literacy (English), students in meaning-driven schools may be engaged in up to three hours of reading, an hour of writing, and ninety minutes of text-based discussion with virtually *no* extra investment of materials or time. Meanwhile students in the typical setting rarely if ever read or write on their own with instruction and for an authentic purpose.

Despite the potentially negative influences of a range of outside factors, teachers and administrators can still make important choices that shape students' literacy experiences for the better. Students can't make the choices to include these non-negotiables in their daily educational experiences, but we can. Let's decide to do it for every reader every day.

POINTS FOR DISCUSSION

1. What parts of your school day are already wrapped in meaning and grounded in purpose?

2. How often do students have the opportunity to read and write for a purpose during the day?
3. How often do they watch an expert reader or writer model the thinking it takes to write in certain formats, genres, or disciplines?
4. What do you view as the major differences between the two columns in tables 8.1 and 8.2?
5. If you were to create a similar chart using examples from your own setting what might you see as the reasons or roadblocks for instruction that would fall in either column?

POINTS TO REMEMBER

1. Nowhere on either the elementary or secondary meaning-driven schedule is there anything that requires more money, time, or special materials.
2. Time spent writing supports reading and learning in general—especially when writing is used in the service of content-specific goals.
3. Time spent reading matters, but the power of that time is dependent on having access to texts students can and want to read, purposes for reading and models of expert reading.

Appendix A

Protocol for Collaboratively Examining Assignments

Modified from a protocol developed by Gene Thompson-Grove, retrieved from: http://schoolreforminitiative.org/doc/examining_assessments.pdf, used with permission.

PURPOSE: TO EXAMINE AN ASSIGNMENT CLOSELY AND DISCUSS ITS IMPLICATIONS

Getting Started

- Identify someone to serve as the facilitator.*
- A designated person in the group brings an example assignment and gives a brief description of the assignment's purpose and context, and answers a few clarifying questions, if necessary.

Describing the Assignment

- The facilitator asks, "What do you see?"
- During this period the group gathers as much information as possible from the assignment. Group members describe what they see, avoiding judgments about the quality of the assignment or interpretations about what the assignment asks students to do. If judgments or interpretations do arise, the facilitator should ask the person to describe the evidence on which they are based. It may be useful to list the group's observations on chart paper. If interpretations come up, they can be listed in another column for later discussion.

Completing the Assignment

- Group members complete (parts of) the assignment.

Interpreting the Assignment

- The facilitator asks, "From the students' perspective, what are they working on as they complete this assignment?"
- The facilitator then asks, "If this assignment was completed successfully by a student, what would it tell us about what this student knows, understands, and is able to do?"
- During this period, the group tries to make sense of what the assignment asks students to do. The group should try to find as many different interpretations as possible. As you listen to each other's interpretations, ask questions that help you better understand each other's perspectives.

Implications for Our Practice

- The facilitator asks, "What are the implications of this work for teaching, learning and assignment?"
- How does this assignment align with your goals for instruction?
- What alternative approaches might address your goals for instruction?
- What teaching and learning issues have been raised for you in terms of your own practice?
- What issues have been raised in terms of schoolwide practices?

Reflecting on the Process

- As a group, share what you have learned.
- Reflect on how well the process worked—what went well, and what could be improved.

Note: According to the School Reform Initiative, "Protocols are most powerful and effective when used within an ongoing professional learning community and facilitated by a skilled facilitator." Please visit the School Reform Initiative's online database to learn more about professional learning communities, protocols and seminars for facilitation: www.schoolreforminitiative.org.

Appendix B

High-Quality Professional Development Selection Criteria

RESEARCH-BASED CHARACTERISTICS OF EXCELLENT PROFESSIONAL DEVELOPMENT

According to a large-scale national study of teacher professional development (Garet et al., 2001) and international comparisons (Darling-Hammond & Richardson, 2009), the following are features of high-quality profession development:

1. Deepens teachers' knowledge of content and how to teach it to students.
2. Provides opportunities for active, hands-on learning.
3. Enables teachers to acquire new knowledge, apply it to practice, and reflect on the results with colleagues.
4. Is coherent with individual teachers' goals and school-wide efforts that links curriculum, assessment, and standards to professional learning.
5. Is collaborative and collegial.
6. Is intensive and sustained over time.

Appendix B

Table B. Professional Development Design Rubric

	Minimal results, possibility of a negative effect on morale	**Possibility of teacher knowledge-building that might transfer to teaching**	**Ideal, with the possibility of developing expertise, encouraging innovation, and supporting student achievement**
Frequency	One-shot workshop	Monthly meetings on a similar topic; workshops with follow-up activities	Multiple, ongoing exposures to the principles and goals (meetings, coaching, reflections), some of which are embedded in the school day
Who's involved?	All full-time staff	Specific groups of teachers	Only those who have collaboratively identified this as an area of interest or area for improvement
Who's the expert?	External visitors who do not have a relationship with the school	Internal presenters only	A combination of internal and outside leaders for sustained leadership and specialized knowledge
What's the focus?	Skill development (training on new methods/ materials)	Exploration of theory OR practice	Contextualized exploration of theory and practice related to collaboratively identified areas for improvement performance
Type of teacher involve-ment	Passive involvement: sit and listen	Involvement including discussion, practice/role play, guided reflection	Active involvement including protocols and other structures for collaborative planning and reflection, action research, peer observations, teacher study groups

Appendix C

Sources for Selecting Series Books

1. GoodReads.com
   http://www.goodreads.com/shelf/show/series
2. Guysread.net
   http://www.guysread.com/books/categories/category/great_series
3. *New York Times* bestsellers list (series books)
   http://www.nytimes.com/best-sellers-books/series-books/list.html
4. Mid-Country Public Libraries
   http://www.mymcpl.org/books-movies-music/juvenile-series
5. Thomas, R., & Catherine B. (2005). *Popular Series Fiction for Middle School and Teen Readers: A Reading and Selection Guide.* Westport, CT: Libraries Unlimited.

Appendix D

Answers to Frequently Asked Questions about Reading Interventions

1. WHERE CAN I FIND OUT IF/HOW A PROGRAM QUALIFIES AS "RESEARCH-BASED"?

The federal government funds a website called the What Works Clearinghouse that reviews scientific studies of programs and interventions using similar criteria as the NRP (http://ies.ed.gov/ncee/wwc/). It will generate lists of programs and rate them based on the strength of the evidence for or against their use.

This site and its methods are not without critics. For example, WWC analysts will not review a study that doesn't meet their criteria because, as they write, "We want to focus on those that make us the most confident that the effect we see is due solely to the intervention alone, and not to the many other factors that are at play in schools and in the lives of students, such as teachers, school, and family."

This type of research "provides causal evidence about the effectiveness of interventions and provides the basis for WWC reports" (WWC, 2012). That's a long way of saying that qualitative studies, single-subject designs, or case studies, no matter how insightful, will never be reviewed. Still, the site offers a perspective that summarizes some of the available research and can be used to peer behind the curtain of ubiquitous "research-based" stickers. The best use of this site is to identify what (if any) studies have been conducted, and review them for the things you care about yourself.

When you read the study yourself weigh things like researcher affiliation, sample size, students included/excluded in the sample, length of the intervention and the researchers' own discussion of their findings.

If it saves you an Internet trip, the only program to ever earn the highest "effectiveness rating" (two plusses) for reading achievement, with medium to large evidence, is Reading Recovery. All others have not been studied with enough rigor and/or have not had robust enough positive results to earn this rating. Some, however have similar high ratings in individual categories like alphabetics, print knowledge, comprehension, etc.

2. WHAT SORT OF CERTIFICATION OR EXPERTISE IS NEEDED TO WORK WITH STRUGGLING READERS OR STUDENTS WITH DISABILITY LABELS?

Reading Recovery teachers are widely considered to be the most expert and most extensively trained, but this training occurs over several years and the program is focused exclusively on first grade. Outside of first grade, teachers and administrators can still take inspiration from the Reading Recovery model of sustained professional development, which includes conducting case studies of individual students, giving and getting feedback on lessons, and engaging with coaches and individual reflection.

Instead of training teachers to perform certain habits and behaviors, Reading Recovery-inspired professional development is focused on creating expert "child-watchers" who can notice, name and extend signs of emerging literacy while identifying strategies to address patterns and specific sources of difficulty. This approach to professional development is not exclusive to Reading Recovery.

For example, we asked fourth grade teachers in a national study of exemplary reading teachers what kind of professional development they valued most; they cited professional development opportunities that helped them see their student's thought processes differently (Gabriel, Day, & Allington, 2010). For some teachers this meant learning an approach that was more student-centered so that the teacher was free to observe students as they worked. For others, it was learning an approach to analyzing student work or patterns of student behavior that provided a new or clearer lens for understanding how children were making sense of instruction. These sorts of professional development experiences draw inspiration from the Reading Recovery's focus on deepening practitioner expertise and could be replicated across settings.

3. IS THERE SUCH A THING AS AN EFFECTIVE COMPUTER PROGRAM INTERVENTION?

According to the What Works Clearinghouse, there isn't. According to common sense about the ability of a machine to provide instruction, no. But, computer tutorial programs may have some incidental benefits that could be used in combination with one-to-one tutoring. These include: access to a bank of interesting, leveled texts; a potentially motivating format and method of tracking progress; flexibility to practice any time, anywhere there is a computer.

Not all computer programs offer these, in fact many only offer stale, contrived texts with mindless click-n-go comprehension questions at the end and "hints" when you click the wrong bubble. When reviewing them for purchase, the diet of texts should be the main concern, followed by the mechanism or incentive to initiate and sustain thoughtful reading.

Computer programs that have registered some degree of success in research studies not reviewed by WWC have likely done so in areas that require practice and repetition (phonics, fluency, scores on multiple choice comprehension tests). Put simply, if a student merely requires more practice and more exposure, a computer can certainly facilitate that. If remediation efforts require specific instruction, strategy building or diagnosis of difficulty, a human (expert) is required.

4. IS DYSLEXIA WORD SCRAMBLING?

The short answer is no. The longer answer is that dyslexia is an umbrella term used to describe difficulty acquiring literacy that cannot be explained by any other factors (e.g., vision, exposure to instruction, other disability). It is also a contested construct with some leaders in neuroscience and literacy research insisting that it exists as a unique and measurable condition, and others pointing out that there is little evidence that there is a distinction between dyslexia and just "garden variety" difficulty with learning to read. Some argue that the label is necessary for services and insurance coverage, and others claim it carries unnecessary assumptions about vision, permanent difficulty, and social stigma.

There is agreement, however, that difficulty learning to read is real and can be painful, but that, label or not, interventions can support literacy acquisition for at least 97 percent of all children (Phillips & Smith, 2010; Torgesen, 2000). The popular notion that dyslexia means students see letters out of order has fueled a number of interventions targeted exclusively at phonics instruction. For some students this amounts to a classic case of perseveration on a weakness, instead of identifying and building upon strengths.

Some others benefit from this kind of instruction and from the practice, exposure and relationships such remediation can provide. It is important to keep in mind, however, that as with all disability labels approaches can and should differ based on the student, not on their label.

5. WHAT IS THE RIGHT SIZE FOR AN INTERVENTION GROUP?

In a study comparing the effect of one-to-one tutoring versus groups of two, three, or five students, all with expert teachers providing a reading intervention, Schwartz, Schmidt, and Lose (2012) found that one-to-one tutoring was significantly more powerful than groups of any size. They also found and that the size of the group (two, three, or five students) didn't matter: small groups of all sizes had a positive effect, but none were as powerful as one-to-one tutoring.

Though Lose (2005) has written that the power in one-to-one settings is the ability of the instructor to identify and build on a reader's strengths, Fitzgerald (2001) has shown that even "minimally trained" (i.e., two weeks of preparation) college student volunteers can have a positive impact on the achievement of at-risk readers in elementary school. It may be that simply providing the time to read and the attention of a caring adult is supportive of growth in and of itself (Klem & Connell, 2004).

6. WHAT ABOUT OUT-OF-SCHOOL READING INTERVENTIONS?

A 2004 meta-analysis of more than forty-seven studies of out-of-school time strategies that addressed reading achievement provides evidence that both after-school and summer school strategies have a positive effect on reading outcomes, especially for lower-achieving students (Miller, Snow, & Lauer, 2004). They also found that elementary students were more likely to demonstrate growth in reading than older students in such settings, though the opposite was true for math achievement in out-of-school settings.

Interestingly, this report also found that programs did not have to have an exclusively academic focus in order to have positive effects on reading achievement. In fact, programs with a social component were just as likely to have a positive impact on reading achievement and more likely to have a positive impact on math achievement. As Rohrbeck et al. (2003) have noted, variety in programming may positively contribute to factors like attendance and engagement.

Researchers conducting this meta-analysis also highlighted the strong effect of programs that included one-to-one tutoring. In fact the largest positive effect size of any of the forty-seven studies came from a study of a one-to-one tutoring program (Leslie, 1998). The positive impact of one-to-one tutoring is indeed a theme across the research on both in- and out-of-school reading interventions (Allington, 2009; Rothman & Henderson, 2011) even for students with learning disability labels (Hock et al., 1995).

Another theme across research on interventions that work in and out of school is the impact of practice and exposure to print. In fact, as Allington et al. (2010) have demonstrated, allowing students to self-select ten books for summer reading had double the effect on reading achievement as attending summer school. That's right, ten choice books give readers better results than several hours a day in a summer school classroom with a teacher. And, this is not the only study that has demonstrated growth in reading as a result of voluntary summer reading programs.

In his review of research on programs that increase access to texts, Lindsay (2010) reported consistently positive effects. Moreover, he found that these effects are strengthened in programs where parents are involved and where texts are distributed over a long period of time instead of all at once. In other words, when it comes to out-of-school reading programs, the evidence strongly suggests: go for it!

References

Allington, R. (2002). *Big brother and the national reading curriculum: How ideology trumped evidence.* Portsmouth, NH: Heinemann.

Allington, R. (2005). Five missing pillars of scientific reading instruction. Retrieved from: http://www.teachersread.net/papers-and-articles

Allington, R. (2009). *What really matters in response to intervention.* Boston: Pearson.

Allington, R., McGill-Franzen, A., Camilli, G., Williams, L., Graff, J., Zeig, J., Zmach, C., & Nowak, R. (2010). Addressing Summer Reading Setback Among Economically Disadvantaged Elementary Students. *Reading Psychology, 31*(5), 411–27.

Altwerger, Bess (2005). *Reading for profit: How the bottom line leaves kids behind.* Portsmouth, NH: Heinemann.

Alvermann, D. (2003). *Seeing themselves as capable and engaged readers: adolescents and re/mediated instruction.* Naperville, IL: Learning Point Associates.

Anderson, R., Hiebert, J., Scott, J., & Wilkinson, I. (1985). *Becoming a nation of readers: The report of the Commission on Reading.* Champaign-Urbana, IL: Center for the Study of Reading.

Anderson, R., Wilson, P., & Fielding, L. (1988). Growth in reading and how children spend their time outside of school. *Reading Research Quarterly, 23,* 285–303.

Applebee, A., Langer, J., Nystrand, M., & Gamoran, A. (2003). Discussion-based approaches to developing understanding: Classroom instruction and student performance in middle and high school English. *American Educational Research Journal, 40*(3), 685–730.

Aylward, E. H., Richards, T. L., Berninger, V. W., Nagy, W. E., Field, K. M., Grimme, A. C., Richards, A. L., Thomson, J. B., & Cramer, S. C. (2003). Instructional treatment associated with changes in brain activation in children with dyslexia. *Neurology, 61*(2), E5–6.

Baldwin, R., Peleg-Bruckner, Z., & McClintock, A. (1985). Effects of topic interest and prior knowledge on reading comprehension. *Reading Research Quarterly, 20,* 497–508.

Bandura, A. (1986). *Social foundations of thought and action: A social cognitive theory.* Englewood Cliffs, NJ: Prentice-Hall.

Beck, I. L., & McKeown, M. G. (2001). Text talk: Capturing the benefits of read-aloud experiences for young children. *The Reading Teacher, 55,* 10–20.

Beck, I., McKeown, M., & Kucan, L. (2002). *Bringing words to life: Robust vocabulary instruction.* New York: Guilford.

Betts, E. A. (1949). Adjusting instruction to individual needs. In N. B. Henry (Ed.), *The forty-eighth yearbook of the National Society for the Study of Education: Part II, Reading in the elementary school* (pp. 266–83). Chicago: University of Chicago Press.

Brenner, D., & Hiebert, E. H. (2010). If I follow the teachers' editions, isn't that enough? Analyzing reading volume in six core reading programs. *Elementary School Journal, 110*(3), 347–63.

Calkins, L. (1992). *The art of teaching reading.* Portsmouth, NH: Heinemann.

Calkins, L. (1994) *The art of teaching writing.* Portsmouth, NH: Heinemann.

Carnell, E. (2005). Boys and their reading: Conceptions of young people about the success of *Full On* magazine. *The Curriculum Journal, 16*(3), 363–89.

Cazden, C. (1988). *Classroom discourse: The language of teaching and learning.* Portsmouth, NH: Heinemann.

Clay, M. (1991). *Becoming literate: The construction of inner control.* Portsmouth, NH: Heinemann.

Collins, A., Brown, J., & Holum, A. (1991). Cognitive apprenticeship: Making thinking visible. *American Educator,* 6-46.

Commeyras, M., & Degroff, L. (1998). Literacy professionals' perspectives on professional development and pedagogy: A United States Survey. *Reading Research Quarterly, 33,* 434-72.

Council on Advancing Adolescent Literacy (2006). *Time to act: An agenda for advancing adolescent literacy for college and career success.* New York: Carnegie Corporation.

Croninger, R., & Valli, L. (2009). "Where's the action?" Challenges to studying the teaching of reading in elementary classrooms. *Educational Researcher, 38*(2), 100–108.

Cunningham, P., & Cunningham, J. (2010). *What really matters in writing: Research-based practices across the elementary curriculum.* Boston: Allyn and Bacon.

Cunningham, A., & Shagoury, R. (2005). *Starting with comprehension: Reading strategies for the youngest learners.* Portland, ME: Stenhouse.

Darling-Hammond, L., and Richardson, N. (2009). Teacher learning: What matters? *Educational Leadership, 66*(5), 46–53.

Deci, E., & Ryan, R. (1985). *Intrinsic motivation and self-determinaton in human behaviour.* New York: Plenum.

Deci, E., & Ryan, R. (2012). About the theory: Self-determination theory, an approach to human motivation and personality. Retrieved from: http://selfdeterminationtheory.org/theory.

Dennis, D. (2009). "I'm not stupid": How assessment drives (in)appropriate reading instruction. *Journal of Adolescent and Adult Literacy , 53* (4), 283–90.

Dudley-Marling, C., & Paugh, P. (2005) The rich get richer; the poor get direct instruction. In B. Altwerger (Ed.) *Reading for profit: How the bottom line leaves kids behind.* Portsmouth, NH: Heinemann.

Duke, N. and Pearson, P. D. (2002). Effective practices for developing reading Comprehension. In Farstrup, A. and Samuels, S.J. (Eds.), *What research has to say about reading Instruction,* 3rd ed., Newark, DE: IRA, pp. 205–42.

Erickson, K. (2000). All children ready to learn: An emergent versus readiness perspective in early literacy. *Seminars in Speech and Language, 21*(3), 193–202.

Fall, R., Webb, N. M., & Chudowsky, N. (2000). Group discussion and large-scale language arts assessment: Effects on students' comprehension. *American Educational Research Journal, 37*(4), 911–41.

Fitzgerald, J. (2001). Can minimally trained college student volunteers help young at-risk children to read better? *Reading Research Quarterly, 36*(1), 28–46.

Frager, A. (2010). Enter the villain: Against oral reading in secondary schools. *American Secondary Education, 38*(3), 28–39.

Freire, P. & Macedo D. (1987). *Literacy: Reading the word and the world.* New York: Routledge & Keegan Paul.

Gabriel, R., Allington, R., & Billlen, M. (2012). Middle schoolers and magazines: what teachers can learn from students' leisure reading habits. *The Clearing House: A Journal of Educational Strategies, Issues and Ideas, 85*(5), 186–91.

Gabriel, R., Day, J., & Allington, R. (2010). What effective teachers taught us about learning to teach effectively. In I. Saleh & M. Khine (Eds.), *Teaching teachers: Approaches in improving quality of education.* Happague, NY: Nova Science Publishers.

Gabrieli, J. (2009). Dyslexia: A new synergy between education and cognitive neuroscience. *Science, 329*(5938), 280–83.

Gallagher, K. (2009). *Readicide*. Portland, ME: Stenhouse.

Gallaudet Research Center (2010). 15 principles for reading to deaf children. Retrieved from: http://www.gallaudet.edu/clerc_center/information_and_resources/info_to_go/language_and_literacy/literacy_at_the_clerc_center/welcome_to_shared_reading_project/15_principles_for_reading_to_deaf_children.html.

Gamoran, A., & Nystrand, M. (1991). Background and instructional effects on achievement on eighth-grade English and social studies. *Journal of Research on Adolescence, 1*, 277–300.

Garan, E. (2002a). *Resisting reading mandates: How to triumph with the truth*. Portsmouth, NH: Heinemann.

Garan, E. (2002b). *Resisting reading mandates*. Portsmouth, NH: Heinemann.

Garan, E. (2004). *In defense of our children: When politics, profit and education collide*. Portsmouth, NH: Heinemann.

Garet, M., Porter, A., Desimone, L., Birman, B., & Yoon, K. (2001). What makes professional development effective? Results from a national sample of teachers. *American Educational Research Journal, 38*(4), 915–45.

Graham, S., & Hebert, M. (2010). *Writing to read: Evidence for how writing can improve reading*. New York: Carnegie Corporation.

Graham, S., & Perin, D. (2007). *Writing next: Effective strategies to improve writing of adolescents in middle and high schools* . New York: Carnegie Corporation.

Guthrie, J. (2002). Preparing students for high-stakes test taking in reading. In A. Farstrup & S. J. Samuels (Eds.), *What research has to say about reading instruction* (pp. 370–91). Newark, DE: International Reading Association.

Guthrie, J., & Humenick, N. (2004). Motivating students to read: Evidence for classroom practices that increase motivation and achievement. In P. D. McCardle & V. Chhabra (Eds.), *The voices of evidence in reading research* (pp. 329–54). Baltimore: Paul H. Brookes Publishing Inc.

Guthrie, J., Wigfield, A., Metsala, J., & Cox, K. (1999). Motivational and cognitive predictors of text comprehension and reading amount. *Scientific Studies of Reading, 3*(3), 231–56.

Hasbrouck, J., & Tindal, G. (2006). Oral reading fluency norms: A valuable assessment tool for reading teachers. *The Reading Teacher, 59*(7), 636–44..

Hock, M. F., Schumaker, J. B., & Deshler, D. D. (1995). Training strategic tutors to enhance learner independence. *Journal of Developmental Education*, 19, 18–26.

Hudson M., & Test D. (2011). Evaluating the evidence base of shared story reading to promote literacy for students with extensive support needs. *Research and Practice for Persons with Severe Disabilities, 36*, 34–45.

Institute of Education Sciences. (2010). What Works Clearinghouse: About us. Retrieved from http://ies.ed.gov/ncee/wwc/aboutus.aspx.

Ivey, G., & Broaddus, K. (2001). Just plain reading: A survey of what makes students want to read in middle schools. *Reading Research Quarterly, 36*, 350–77.

Johnston, P. (2005). Literacy assessment and the future. *The Reading Teacher, 58*(7), 66–68.

Keller, T. A., & Just, M. A. (2009). Altering cortical activity: Remediation-induced changes in the white matter of poor readers. *Neuron, 64*(5), 624–31.

Kelley, M. J., & Clausen-Grace, N. (2006). R⁵: The sustained silent reading makeover that transformed readers. *The Reading Teacher, 60*, 148–56.

Klem, M. & Connell, J. (2004). Relationships matter: Linking teacher support to student engagement and achievement. *Journal of School Health, 74*, 262–73.

Knapp, M. S., & Associates. (1995). *Teaching for meaning in high-poverty classrooms*. New York: Teachers College Press.

Knowles, M. (1990). *The adult learner. A neglected species, fourth edition*. Houston: Gulf Publishing.

Langer, J. A. (2001). Beating the odds: Teaching middle and high school students to read and write well. *American Educational Research Journal, 38*(4), 837–80.

Langer, J., & Applebee, A. (1986). Reading and writing instruction: Toward a theory of teaching and learning. *Review of Research in Education, 13*, 171–94.

Lave, J., & Wenger, E. (1991). *Situated learning: Legitimate peripheral participation.* Cambridge, UK: Cambridge University Press.

Leslie, A. (1998). The effects of an afterschool tutorial program on the reading and mathematics achievement, failure rate, and discipline referral rate of students in a rural middle school (rural education). (Doctoral dissertation, University of Georgia, 1998). *Dissertation Abstracts International, 59,* 06A.

Lindsay, J. (2010). *Children's access to print material and education-related outcomes: Findings from a meta-analytic review.* Naperville, IL: Learning Point Associates.

Lindsay, J. (2013). Impacts of interventions that increase children's access to print material. In R. L. Allington & A. McGill-Franzen (Eds.), *Summer reading: Closing the rich/poor reading achievement gap.* New York: Teachers College Press.

Magazine Publishers of America. (2004). *Teen market profile.* New York: Magazine Publishers of America.

Mallette, M. H., Readence, J. E., McKinney, M., & Smith, M. M. (2000). A critical analysis of two preservice teachers' knowledge of struggling readers: Raced, classed, and gendered? *Reading Research and Instruction, 39,* 222–34.

Malloy, J. A., & Gambrell, L. B. (2010). New insights on motivation in the literacy classroom. In J. A. Malloy, B. A. Marinak, & L. B. Gambrell (Eds.), *Essential readings on motivation* (pp. 163–72). Newark, DE: International Reading Association.

McGill-Franzen, A. (2007). *Kindergarten Literacy.* New York: Scholastic.

McGill-Franzen, A. (2010). Series books for young readers: Seeking reading pleasure and developing reading competence. In D. Wooten & B. Cullinan (Eds.), *Children's literature in the reading program: An invitation to read* (pp. 57–65). Newark: DE, International Reading Association.

McGill-Franzen, A., & Allington, R. (1990). Comprehension and coherence: Neglected elements of literacy instruction in remedial and resource room services. *Journal of Reading, Writing, and Learning Disabilities, 6,* 149–80

McGill-Franzen, A., Allington, R., Yokoi, L., & Brooks, G. (1999). Putting books in the classroom seems necessary but not sufficient. *Journal of Educational Research, 93*(2), 67–74.

McGraw Hill. (2012). About us. Retrieved from: http://www.mcgraw-hill.com/site/about-us.

McKinney, J. (1989). Longitudinal research on the behavioral characteristics of children with learning disabilities. *Journal of Learning Disabilities, 22*(3), 141–50.

Mehan, H. (1979). *Learning lessons: Social organization in the classroom.* Cambridge, MA: Harvard University Press.

Miller, D. (2012). Guess my lexile? *Education Week Teacher.* Retrieved from: http://blogs.edweek.org/teachers/book_whisperer/2012/07/guess_my_lexile.html.

Miller, K., Snow, D., & Lauer, P. (2004). *Noteworthy perspectives: Out-of-school time programs for at-risk students.* Aurora, CO: McREL.

Moje, E. B. (2008). The complex world of adolescent literacy: Myths, motivations, and mysteries. *Harvard Educational Review,* Spring 2008, 107–54.

National Educators Association. (2012). Reading yesterday and today: The NRP report and other factors. Retrieved from: http://www.nea.org/readingupdates.

National Reading Panel. (2000). *Teaching children to read: An evidence-based assessment of the scientific research literature on reading and its implications for reading instruction.* Rockville, MD: National Institutes of Child Health and Human Development. Retrieved from www.nationalreadingpanel.org/publications/summary.htm

National Study of School Engagement. (2012). Retrieved from: http://nsse.iub.edu/html/about.cfm.

Netz, H. (2012). Gifted conversations: discursive patterns in gifted classes. Paper presented at the Discourse Analysis and Rhetoric Group Anniversary Conference, Loughborough, UK.

No Child Left Behind Act of 2001, 20 U.S.C. § 6319 (2008).

Nye, B., Konstantopoulos, S., & Hedges, L. (2004). How large are teacher effects? *Educational Evaluation and Policy Analysis, 26*(3), 237–54.

Nystrand, M. (2006). Research on the role of classroom discourse as it affects reading comprehension. *Research in the Teaching of English, 40,* 392–412.

Nystrand, M. , & Gamoran, A. (1991) Instructional discourse, student engagement, and literature achievement. *Research in the Teaching of English, 25*, 261–90.

O'Connor, R. E., Bell, K. M., Harty, K. R., Larkin, L. K., Sackor, S. M., & Zigmond, N. (2002). Teaching reading to poor readers in the intermediate grades: A comparison of text difficulty. *Journal of Educational Psychology, 94*(3), 474–85.

Paris, S. (2005). Reinterpreting the development of reading skills. *Reading Research Quarterly, 20*(2), 184–202.

Phillips, G., & Smith, P. (1997). A third chance to learn: The development and evaluation of specific interventions for young children experiencing difficulty in learning to read. Wellington: New Zealand Council for Educational Research.

Phillips, G., & Smith, P. (2010). Closing the gaps: Literacy for the hardest to teach. In P. Johnston (Ed.), *RTI in literacy: Responsive and comprehensive* (pp. 219–46). Newark, DE: International Reading Association.

Phillips, L. M., Hayward, D. V., & Norris, S. P. (2011). Persistent reading disabilities: Challenging six erroneous beliefs. In A. McGill-Franzen & R. Allington (Eds.), *The Handbook of Reading Disability Research* (pp. 110–19). New York: Routledge.

Pressley, M., Allington, R., Wharton-McDonald, R., Block, C. C., & Morrow, L. M. (2001). *Learning to read: Lessons from exemplary first grade classrooms.* New York: Guilford Press.

Pugh, K. (2011, October). *Advances in understanding how the brain reads.* Presentation at the Haskins Training Institute Educational Conference: Reading, language and the brain: Understanding the development of literacy, New Haven, CT.

Purcell-Gates, V. (1997). *Other people's words: The cycle of low literacy.* Cambridge, MA: Harvard University Press.

Rasinski, T. (n.d.). Effective teaching of reading from phonics to fluency. Retrieved June 2010 from http://www.timrasinski.com/presentations/effective_teaching_of_reading-from_phonics_to_fluency_2009.pdf/.

Richardson, V., Anders, P., Tidwell, D., & Loyd, C. (1991). The relationship between teachers' beliefs and practices in reading comprehension instruction. *American Educational Research Journal, 28*(3), 559–86.

Rohrbeck, C. A., Ginsburg-Block, M. D., Fantuzzo, J. W., & Miller, T. R. (2003). Peer-assisted learning interventions with elementary school students: A meta-analytic review. *Journal of Educational Psycholog, 95*, 77–89.

Rothman, T., & Henderson, M. (2011). Do school-based tutoring programs significantly improve student performance on standardized tests? *Research in Middle Level Education, 24*(6), 1–10.

Scanlon, D. M., & Sweeney, J.M. (2010). Kindergarten intervention: Teaching to prevent reading difficulties. In P. Johnston (Ed.), *RTI in literacy: Responsive and comprehensive.* Newark, DE: International Reading Association.

Scharlach, T. D. (2008). These kids just aren't motivated to read: The influence of pre-service teachers' beliefs on their expectations, instruction, and evaluation of struggling readers. *Literacy Research and Instruction, 47*(3), 158–73.

Schleper, D. R. (1997). *Reading to deaf children: Learning from deaf adults.* Washington, DC: Laurent Clerc National Deaf Education Center at Gallaudet University.

Schwartz, R., Schmidt, M., and Lose, M. (2012) Effects of teacher-student ratio in response to intervention approaches. *The Elementary School Journal, 112*(4), 547–67.

Shanahan, T. (2003). Research-based reading instruction: Myths about the National Reading Panel report: *The Reading Teacher, 56*, 646–55.

Shanahan, T. (2011). Center for Development and Learning. Retrieved from: http://www.cdl.org/resource-library/articles/common-core-vs-guided-reading.php?type=recent&id=Yes.

Shaywitz, S., & Shaywitz, B. (2007). What neuroscience really tells us about reading instruction: A response to Judy Willis. *Educational Leadership, 64*(5), 74–76.

Shaywitz, B., Shaywitz, S., Blachman, B., Pugh, K., Fulbright, R. K., Skudlarski, P., et al. (2003). Development of left occipto-temporal systems for skilled reading in children after phonologically based intervention. *Biological Psychiatry, 55*(9), 926–33.

Snow, C. (2002). Reading for understanding: Toward an R&D program in reading comprehension. Santa Monica, CA: RAND Corporation.

Spear-Swerling, L., & Sternberg, R. J. (1996). *Off track: When poor readers become "learning disabled."* Boulder, CO: Westview Press.

Stanovich, Keith E. (1986). Matthew effects inreading: Some consequences of individual differences in the acquisition of literacy. *Reading Research Quarterly, 21*(4), 360–407.

Swanson, E., Vaughn, S., Wanzek., Petscher, Y., Heckert, J., Cavanaugh, C., Kraft, G., & Tackett, K. (2011). A synthesis of read-aloud interventions on early reading outcomes among preschool through third graders at risk for reading difficulties. *Journal of Learning Disabilities, 44*(3), 258–75.

Tatum, A. W. (2009). *Reading for their life: (Re)building the textual lineages of African American adolescent males.* Portsmouth, NH: Heinemann.

Taylor, B. M., & Pearson, P. D. (Eds.) (2002). *Teaching reading: Effective schools, accomplished teachers.* Mahwah, NJ: Lawrence Erlbaum.

Taylor, B. M., Pearson, P. D., Peterson, D. S., & Rodriguez, M. C. (2003). Reading growth in high-poverty classrooms: The influence of teacher practices that encourage cognitive engagement in literacy learning. *Elementary School Journal, 104*, 3–28.

Teale, W. H., & Sulzby, E. (1986). *Emergent literacy: Writing and reading.* Norwood, NJ: Ablex.

Thornburg, D. (1993). Intergenerational literacy learning with bilingual families: A context for the analysis of social mediation of thought. *Journal of Literacy Research, 25*, 323.

Torgesen, J. (2000). Individual differences in response to early interventions in reading: The lingering problem of treatment resisters. *Learning Disabilities Research and Practice, 15*(1), 55–64.

Torgesen, J. K., Alexander, A. W., Wagner, R. K., Rashotte, C. A., Voeller, K., Conway, T., et al. (2001). Intensive remedial instruction for children with severe reading disabilities: Immediate and long-term outcomes from two instructional approaches. *Journal of Learning Disabilities, 34*, 33–58.

Torgesen, J. (2006). Recent discoveries from research on remedial interventions for children with dyslexia. In M. Snowling and C. Hulme (Eds.), *The science of reading: A handbook* (pp. 521–37). Oxford: Blackwell Publishers.

Valencia, S., Place, N., Martin, S., & Grossman, P. (2006). Curriculum materials for elementary reading: Shackles and scaffolds for four beginning teachers. *The Elementary School Journal, 107*(1), 93–120.

Valencia, S., & Riddle-Buly, M. (2004). Behind test scores: What struggling readers really need. *The Reading Teacher, 57*, 520–33.

Vellutino, F., Scanlon, D., Small, S., & Fanueuel, D. (2006). Response to Intervention as a vehicle for distinguishing between children with and without reading disabilities: Evidence for the role of kindergarten and first-grade interventions. *Journal of Learning Disabilities, 29*(2), 157–69.

Vroom, V. (1964). *Work and motivation.* New York: Wiley.

Vygotsky L. (1978). *Mind in society: The development of higher psychological processes.* Cambridge, MA: Harvard University Press.

What Works Clearinghouse. (2012). Find what works. Retrieved from http://ies.ed.gov/ncee/wwc/findwhatworks.aspx.

Winfield, L. F. (1986). Teacher beliefs toward academically at risk students in inner urban schools. *Urban Review*, 18(4), 253–68.

About the Author

Rachael Gabriel is assistant professor of reading education at the University of Connecticut. Rachael's career in education began as a middle school literacy teacher in an urban charter school. She has since worked as a literacy specialist, reading therapist, and teacher mentor. She holds a PhD in education with a focus on literacy studies and graduate certificates in both quantitative and qualitative research methods in education. Rachael currently teaches courses in reading methods, assessment, and program design, and literacy in the content areas. A former fellow of the Baker Center for Public Policy at the University of Tennessee, Rachael is now an associate of the Center for Education Policy Analysis at the University of Connecticut, where she studies teacher evaluation policies and the role of discourse in literacy classrooms.

As a researcher, Rachael has focused on literacy instruction as well as teacher preparation, development, and evaluation, with a specific interest in related policy issues. Her research most often lies at the intersections of literacy instruction, teacher development, and evaluation, with issues of equity, access, and social justice. Rachael's research has appeared in a range of journals and edited volumes published within and outside of the United States. She is the author of *Reading 's Non-Negotiables: Elements of Effective Instruction* and contributing author and editor of *Performances of Research: Critical issues in K – 12 education.* She currently serves as the editor of the online journal *Catalyst: A Social Justice Forum.*